THE FUNDAMENTAL SOCIAL LAW

COSMAS AND DAMIAN
Freely you have received, freely give.
Take neither gold, nor silver, nor copper in your purses,
nor a bag for your journey ... (MT. 10: 8-10)

The
Fundamental Social Law

Rudolf Steiner on the Work of the

Individual and the Spirit of Community

Peter Selg

2011
STEINERBOOKS

SteinerBooks
610 Main Street, Great Barrington, MA 01230
www.steinerbooks.org

Translated by Catherine E. Creeger.

Originally published in German as *Die Arbeit des Einzelnen
und der Geist der Gemeinschaft. Rudolf Steiner und das "Soziale
Hauptgesetz"* by Verlag am Goetheanum, Dornach, Switzerland 2007.

Library of Congress Cataloging-in-Publication Data

Selg, Peter, 1963-
  [Arbeit des Einzelnen und der Geist der Gemeinschaft. English]
  The fundamental social law : Rudolf Steiner on the work of the
individual and the spirit of community / Peter Selg.
     p. cm.
Includes bibliographical references.
ISBN 978-0-88010-654-2
1. Steiner, Rudolf, 1861-1925. 2. Economics – Religious
aspects – Anthroposophy. 3. Religion and social sciences. 4.
Anthroposophy – Doctrines I. Title.
BP596.E25S45 2011
299'.935—dc23
                     2011030695

Contents

Most of all, however, our times are suffering from the lack of any basic social understanding of how work can be incorporated into the social organism correctly, so that everything we do is truly performed for the sake of our fellow human beings. We can acquire this understanding only by learning to really insert our "I" into the human community. New social forms will not be provided by nature but can emerge only from the human "I" through real, person-to-person understanding — that is, when the needs of others become a matter of direct experience for us.

RUDOLF STEINER, JUNE 9, 1922 (83, 245[1])

Introduction

This is what is needed: we must rise to the occasion and summon the inner courage to think radically in certain matters, as our times demand of any alert individual.

— Rudolf Steiner, (333, 27)

We must hope for ever-increasing understanding of these matters.

— Rudolf Steiner, (340, 40)

THIS STUDY EXPANDS and elaborates on a lecture entitled "Spiritual Science and Social Issues: Rudolf Steiner and the Fundamental Social Law," which I gave on April 29, 2006, at the general meeting of the *Freien Gemeinschaftsbank* [Independent Community Bank] in Basel, Switzerland.

That lecture described the main features, background, and purpose of the "fundamental social law," which Rudolf Steiner formulated for the first time around the turn of the year 1905/06. Steiner's seemingly simple *"social axiom"* (185a) or *"basic principle of social science and societal activity"* (186) posits separating the performance of human work from material compensation: "It is essential to avoid associating the concept of work in any way...with the concept of income" (332a). More than a century has elapsed since Steiner's idea first appeared in a small theosophical journal, but the perspectives he formulated there and developed in various ways in his later work seem to have lost little of their relevance. The replacement of human labor by technology has made unemployment a global problem and has provoked an existential crisis of meaning among individuals deprived of tasks in life. This situation, along with the world-wide proliferation of power, egotism, violence, and destructivity, is now prompting us to rethink many of our economic and social ideas, especially the mainstream understanding of work, competition, and remuneration.[2] "Most of all, however, our times are suffering from the lack of any basic social understanding of how work can be incorporated into the social body correctly" (183). Ever since Adam Smith, most thinking about the market economy has been based on the premise that maximally enhanced self-interest is the most efficient motivator of economic production, universal prosperity, and social welfare; furthermore, egotistical desire for profit is the only possible basis for the human urge to work. (In Smith's words, "We appeal not to your human kindness but to your self-interest.") Developments that have ensued since Smith's time, however, clearly call for revision of some largely unquestioned paradigms—along with acknowledgment of the actual situation, which Rudolf Steiner described in these words as early as 1908: "Nonetheless, it is true that all of today's admirable inner and outer technical and scientific accomplishments have remained unmatched by our societal activity and social structures" (56).

*

Rudolf Steiner did not formulate utopian ideals or postulate moral dogmas; his sober analysis of the contemporary situation was more anthropological in character. He argued emphatically that "solutions" to "social issues"—already the subject of much discussion in the early years of the twentieth century—would not emerge from economic theorizing but would have to involve reflection on the nature of the human being, human work, society, and the social body. If we misunderstand Rudolf Steiner and the quality of the anthroposophical spiritual science he founded, we may easily dismiss such reflection as either outdated or long since accomplished on the academic level, but in reality it is still only in its earliest beginnings in many places. In the history of science, this phenomenon is related to the structural principles of paradigm formation and maintenance.[3] On the level of partisan psychology, it has to do with a "flight from and fear of ideas" (24); on the institutional level, with a real lack of truly independent, objective academic science or epistemological study with no ties to any specific industry or vested interest:"

> Let us consider, for example, the relationship between science and religion or theology. In medieval cultural and intellectual history, we often encounter the statement that philosophy, as worldly wisdom, is theology's "train-bearer." In modern times, we believe that this situation has changed, and indeed it has, but how? The worldly sciences have become the servants of worldly powers, of nations and economic cycles. To tell the truth, this has not been a change for the better[4] (329).

In the first two decades of the twentieth century, Rudolf Steiner was already describing the "error" of believing that *"salvation can come only from the economy"* (330.) In the decades since then, the phenomenon he described as an evolution dominated (if not wholly determined) by technological and economic perspectives has produced an ever more one-sided situation, along with crises that have increasingly left their stamp on international political constellations and on our civilization as a whole. Right up to the present day, wars have been declared and waged on the basis of economic and political interests. The legal forms and instruments of nations have been misused, nature's kingdoms have been abused and extirpated, and public affairs—and education—have been subjected to the dictates of technology and economics, and, de facto, aligned with them. *"In modern times, as if hypnotized by economic activity and age-old habitual thinking"* (328, 35), many proposals for "reform"—whether with regard to labor market policy or social therapy—follow well-trodden, inherently conventional paths that allow the problems to become ingrained, increasing not only cultural stagnation and destruction but also resignation on the part of individuals.

"The question of the meaning of human labor underlies everything," said Rudolf Steiner at the beginning of the twentieth century (328, 190). His "fundamental social law"—and in fact, all of his thoughts on the terms and conditions of economic and public activity—were totally new, unaccustomed, challenging, and ahead of their time. Although in many of his presentations on the "fundamental social law" and the "threefold social organism," Steiner made the case for them purely in terms of political economy, those familiar with all of his work cannot fail to notice how far-reaching and fundamental the perspectives he represented actually were (and still are).

Steiner's explanations of "the fundamental social law" clearly come at a crossroad in the cultural development of civilization. They suggest a practical route to new forms of society and community that leave the pathological spirals of egotism and destructive materialism behind and give expression to a higher humanity—and even to an effective "Christ Impulse," as Steiner calls it. As such, they stand under the sign of a future culture of selflessness that is by no means ascetic or moralistic in character but is based instead on enhanced human forces of individuality and social conscience and therefore allows for the evolution of individual consciousness.[5] This future culture—based on truly independent spiritual activity that supports the appropriate upbringing, schooling, and advancement of individuals—will have to produce specific changes in the structures of our public and working lives (now corrupt for the most part). Meanwhile, it must also be prepared to resonate behind the scenes of current discussions about a basic guaranteed income.[6] This future culture is already making its first appearances in many places.

*

In spite of many depressing experiences (even in anthroposophical settings) and the relatively minimal reception his social impulses encountered during his lifetime, Rudolf Steiner never allowed his intentions to falter. He said:

> If we are to contribute at all to human salvation, we must not be pessimistic; we must believe in our work. We must have the courage to believe we are really capable of bringing about what we think is right. To me, it sounds self-destructive to say, "We have ideas that could be put into practice, but I don't believe that's possible." The question is not whether our ideas correspond to reality but simply how to implement them. Instead of thinking about the state of people's heads today, we should think about what they must become. (330, 54)

On balance, even eighty years after Steiner's death (and in spite of all protestations to the contrary), anthroposophical efforts to model the implementation of the fundamental social law and social threefoldness are only modestly encouraging. ("If we had just a hundred institutions today that had truly incorporated the anthroposophical social impulse on the structural level, the world would look quite different."[7]) Many promising beginnings are counterbalanced by failed attempts, and even where encouraging early breakthroughs occurred, later developments reversed them and led to a partial loss of what had already been achieved (as in the Camphill Movement). Clearly, such situations are due in part to inadequate understanding or over/under/misinterpretation of what Steiner meant.[8] In addition, it has become obvious that in all such attempts, the level of consciousness of those involved is crucial, as is their connection (voluntarily achieved) to the "spirit of the totality," whose real presence Rudolf Steiner linked to the success of any alternative to egotism as the incentive for work:

Individuals who work for another person must see their reason and motivation for work in that person. Similarly, anyone who works for the totality must be able to sense the value, the essence, and the importance of that totality, which is possible only if the totality is something very different from a more or less indeterminate sum of individuals. It must be filled with a real spirit in which each individual can participate. Each one must be able to acknowledge the rightness of the whole and want it to be as it is. The totality must have a spiritual mission, and each individual must want to contribute to fulfilling that mission. [...] Right into the details, the spirit of the totality must be alive. (34, 24f.).

A number of different anthroposophical institutions have experienced that when anthroposophy (formerly a vital and integral element of their "totality" and "spiritual mission") became diluted, they also began to fail as social models. It seems that whenever the "spirit of the totality," the spirituality and ideal intention of common effort, was no longer strongly and concretely present in the individuals involved but had been replaced by nothing more than a vague, indecisive, noncommittally stated and publicly proclaimed "openness" to "anthroposophy" (or "spirituality"), it was no longer possible to find one's "reason for work" in the other and in the community. Rudolf Steiner calls this "the non-Christian principle of opportunism" (175, 250).

Regrettable as this development may seem, it remains a consequence of spiritual realities, and if received and understood positively, it results in a clear need to take up spiritual-scientific work and spiritual training anew and to tackle specific tasks for the future without making concessions to the supposed spirit of the times. At the same time, however, we must not lose sight of the fact that even in the twenty-first century, we are still not dealing with ultimate or ideal solutions but with ever-changing attempts to *"steer ... "existence in a social direction."* As Steiner puts it,

The "social question" that is now emerging in human life cannot be solved by a few individuals or by parliaments. That cannot and will not happen. It is a component of modern civilization as such, and now that it has appeared, it will persist. It will need to be solved anew in every moment in the world's history and evolution. Human life has recently entered a stage that repeatedly allows the antisocial element to emerge from social arrangements and establishments, and this antisocial element will always have to be tackled anew. Just as an organism always grows hungry again after a period of satiety, so too the social body repeatedly enters a disordered state after a period of well-ordered affairs. Just as there is no nourishment that satiates permanently, there is also no universal remedy that can ensure lasting order in social conditions. Nonetheless, human beings can establish communities in which the living interactions of individuals can repeatedly steer their existence in a social direction. (23, 14f.)

Consider the global state of civilization at the beginning of the twenty-first century: Advanced and inherently powerful technology dominates human consciousness through media-engendered needs. The compulsion to consume is maximized, self-interest prevails, and human soul forces have definitely weakened.[9] We have reason to question whether this situation could actually still permit the social developments Rudolf Steiner spoke about in the first two decades of the twentieth century. In the face of fateful economic, cultural, and social developments, Steiner spent his last, almost desperate years of work on a breakthrough that was then still barely possible (and ultimately failed). If nothing else, the signature of this work speaks a very different language.[10] We can be certain that the task of *"steering" existence in a social direction"* and *"developing truly social thinking"* (23, 192) remains as important as ever, on both the large scale and the small. Also still applicable are Rudolf

Steiner's previously cited words, prototypically Christian in substance:

> We must have the courage to believe we are really capable of bringing about what we think is right. To me, it sounds self-destructive to say, "We have ideas that could be put into practice, but I don't believe that's possible [any more]."[11]

*

For the opportunity to write up this study, I am grateful to Markus Jermann and the Freien Gemeinschaftsbank [Independent Community Bank] of Basel and to the many friends and supporters of the Ita Wegman Institute for Basic Research into Anthroposophy, including the foundations that fund the Institute's spiritual work (Software AG-Stiftung, Christophorus-Stiftung, Zukunftsstiftung Gesundheit, Zukunftsstiftung Soziales Leben.) My personal thanks go out to Dr. Peter Schnell of Darmstadt, Dr. Georg and Mr. Niklaus Müller of Zurich, and my colleague Lüder Jachens of Stiefelhofen for their significant involvement in this project.

PETER SELG

Director of the Ita Wegman Institute
for Basic Research into Anthroposophy
Arlesheim, November 2006

1.

Rudolf Steiner, Berlin, and the Beginning of the Twentieth Century

I will serve the [workers' education] school until they no longer want me....

— RUDOLF STEINER, OCTOBER 2, 1903 (39, 432)

For several reasons, [the spiritual scientific movement] cannot show itself now in the face it will wear someday. One reason is that in order to first gain a foothold, it must address a particular group of people. [...] To the extent that suitable circumstances ensue, spiritual science will also find forms of expression that allow it to speak to other circles.

— RUDOLF STEINER, 1905 (34, 220)

As we work our way through spiritual scientific ideas, we enhance our capacity for social action. In this sense, it is important not only *which* thoughts we take in through spiritual science, but *what we do with our thinking as a result.*

— Rudolf Steiner, 1905 (34, 196)

W HEN THE FIRST PART OF HIS FUNDAMENTAL ESSAY, "The Social Question and Theosophy," appeared in the magazine *Lucifer-Gnosis*, which he edited, Rudolf Steiner was forty-five years old. For more than three years, the philosopher, Goethe researcher, and cultural critic from Vienna had headed the work of the German Section of the Theosophical Society. In this context, his research remained relatively obscure and little known to the general public. In the Theosophical Society, Rudolf Steiner accompanied and encouraged many pupils on their paths of esoteric development. His work as a spiritual teacher consisted in presenting content and concrete exercises in concentration and mediation. In a letter accepting this position in the summer of 1902, Rudolf Steiner had written, "I will build on the strength that enables me to introduce '*students of spirit*' to the path of development. That must be the sole significance of my inauguration" (260a, 89).

From the very beginning and in spite of these spiritual and esoteric intentions, Rudolf Steiner's work on behalf of theosophical spiritual science—like his previous publishing and cultural activities in Vienna, Weimar, and Berlin—also had a public aspect. Already shortly after accepting the position of general secretary of the German section of the Theosophical Society, Steiner began giving public lectures in the Berlin House of Architects, a building where large public events were held. In 1905, for example, in addition to nine lectures on Schiller at the Free University in Berlin, he gave four academically oriented lectures in the House of Architects that were intended to show the connection between theosophical spiritual science and the four classical faculties of theology, jurisprudence, medicine, and philosophy. For Steiner—in contrast to the prevailing introverted bourgeois tendencies within the Theosophical Society—the social relevance of the spiritual teachings he represented was essential, as he had already made clear in 1903 (the first year of the publication of the journal *Lucifer-Gnosis*) in his essay "Theosophy and Socialism," in which he had attempted to demonstrate the extent to which theosophy would have to contribute to shaping social conditions in the future. In fact, he wrote, it must become the "soul of all things social" (344, 439). He continued:

> There may well be some theosophists who want to remain remote from the world and constantly repeat the statement that it is the destiny (karma) of modern peoples to face the test of their purely material outlook. To this we must respond that while disease is certainly a sick person's destiny, those called upon to be healers are neglecting their duty if they avoid all attempts to heal because they see illness as a test. (34, 440)

*

Rudolf Steiner began publishing his essay "The Social Question and Theosophy" at the end of 1905, a year of international political crises and tests, especially due to changes in Russia. At the same time as major strikes by miners in the West

German Ruhr area, the Russian strikers' movement achieved revolutionary dynamics with "Bloody Sunday" in St. Petersburg, leading to the initial creation of socialist forms of organization. In the autumn of 1905, Russian workers proclaimed a general strike; on October 26, the first soviet was formed. That same day, in an urgent lecture on "Theosophy and the Social Question" in the Berlin House of Architects, Rudolf Steiner gave his first oral presentation of the basic premises of the essay that would appear in print two months later.[12]

In January of 1905, Rudolf Steiner had been forced—against his will and under considerable pressure from the school's socialist leadership—to give up his long-standing and highly successful teaching activity at the Berlin Workers' School. To Marie von Sivers, his colleague and future spouse, Steiner wrote, "You know that I saw a mission in my activity in these circles. Here something has really been destroyed that I did not want to see destroyed" (262, 88). Steiner had joined the school's faculty five and a half years earlier, in the autumn of 1899, at the request of the school's administration and on the recommendation of socialist Kurt Eisner.[13] The school had been founded by Wilhelm Liebknecht in the early 1890s. Liebknecht, who belonged to the generation of Steiner's parents, was a member of the German Reichstag [parliament] and editor-in-chief of the Social Democratic newspaper *Vorwärts* [*Onward!*] Shortly after beginning his activity in the German empire's capital, Liebknecht had given his famous lecture "Knowledge is Power," placing emphatic priority on a proletarian educational policy for the proletariat under circumstances that continued to uphold knowledge as an exclusive privilege of the bourgeoisie:

> In parliament, Count Kanitz had said that it was enough for the lower classes to learn to read and write a little and do just enough arithmetic to count their daily wages. On a schoolhouse wall on a large property in the city of Berlin was inscribed in letters of gold, "Loving Christ is better

than all knowledge." That was the basic principle of primary education in the empire's capital. Book learning was just adequate for acquiring a handyman's skills.[14]

The classes of the Workers' School were held in a small room in a pub in the southeastern part of the city from nine to eleven at night, after the end of the students' long work day. Their studies emphasized political economy but also included history, law, and natural history, and they were expected to practice oral and written communication. Their readiness to participate in this demanding course of study was quite remarkable.[15] In the words of Rudolf Steiner as a contemporary witness:

> You should have seen for yourselves how for decades the proletariat assembled in the evenings, in hours wrested from heavy work, to be instructed in modern economics, on the importance of work, capital, and the consumption and production of goods. You should have seen the tremendous desire for education that most of these proletarian individuals developed, pursuing knowledge at a time when, on the other side of the great divide, the higher classes were going to the theater or devoting themselves to other diversions, casting at most an occasional glance from on high at the misery of the proletariat. (333, 18)

Rudolf Steiner, himself of lower class origins, never denied his family's background. In a different connection, he said:

> Actually, I come from proletarian circles myself, and I can still remember looking out the window as a child and seeing the first Austrian Social Democrats passing by in their big hats, on their way to their first Austrian assembly in the nearby woods. Most of them were miners. From then on, I was actually able to witness everything that played out in the Socialist movement [...] as it appeared to someone

destined to think not only *about* the proletariat, but *with* the proletariat, while at the same time preserving an independent view of life and all its various facets. Perhaps that was my testimony in 1892, when I wrote my *Philosophy of Spiritual Activity*, which truly advocated for the social structures I now see as necessary for developing human talents. (330, 43)

The Marxist Rosa Luxemburg had categorically refused to be part of the faculty of the Berlin Workers' School. "Although naturally drawn to teaching, she turned down this opportunity because of her extremely one-sided position within the Socialist movement, in the effort to avoid any allegation of recruiting willing followers from among the unspoiled and uncritical youth. For the same reason, she refused to give even a single lecture." Unlike Rosa Luxemburg, Rudolf Steiner was in some ways diametrically opposed to the school's socialist orientation, yet in the autumn of 1899 he spontaneously agreed to teach history there:

> I had little interest in the school's socialist connections. [...] I told its board of directors that if I were to teach there, I would lecture on history according to my own ideas on the course of humanity's evolution, not in the Marxist style now customary in Social Democratic circles. They continued to want my services. For me, the school consisted of men and women from the proletariat; the fact that most of them were Social Democrats was of no concern to me. (28, 375)

Karl Liebknecht, who was no longer active in the School's administration due to advanced age (in fact, he was close to death), had nothing against Steiner's appointment and teaching activity: "You should be glad to have such a good teacher; his political views are none of your business."[17] Having been guaranteed the freedom to teach as he chose, Steiner began giving lessons toward the end of 1899 with a lecture course on "Spiritual Streams in History: From the Reformation to the French Revolution." His lecture courses were soon extraordinarily well-attended, ultimately drawing more than two hundred listeners. He went on to cover the French Revolution and nineteenth-century industrialism, and later added evening sessions devoted to the history of literature, culture, and philosophy, which he presented with great dedication. On Sunday evenings, he read selections by various poets and talked about their biographies. One member of the audience recalls:

> He [Rudolf Steiner] also always pointed out the social and political tensions that broke through in this poetry. For him, what spoke out of these verses was the spirit of revolution, the heated intentions of outrage against the narrow-minded attitudes and incurable shortsightedness of the bourgeoisie, and the acknowledgment—born of spiritual vision—of the need (and here again he quoted Marx) to change the world. He was the one who always taught us that it is up to us to shape our lives according to our insights.[18]

After Rudolf Steiner's lectures, there were always long discussions that lasted until after midnight. Increasingly, they also touched on issues involving individual problems and philosophies of life:

> "Why is there so little happiness in life, when everyone just wants to be happy?" Dr. Steiner replied, "Well, maybe being happy is not our reason for being alive!"
> "But what else could life be for?" the young man asked, shocked. "Well, just assume for a moment that we are alive so we can accomplish some particular task."[19]

Rudolf Steiner at the Workers' School. Berlin, 1900

Steiner's words resonated so well with his working-class audience that he became one of the most sought-after speakers at union events in Berlin. He spoke to printers, metalworkers, and streetcar workers, among others, and was unquestionably the most important faculty member of the school founded by Liebknecht.

Although materially in need himself, Rudolf Steiner categorically refused increased remuneration for his lectures at the school. He often attended the school's board meetings as a faculty representative, and a participant in one such meeting recalls a conversation with Steiner about payment:

> As Dr. Rudolf Steiner's lecture courses on literature and history became increasingly popular, the school's board of directors discussed the possibility of paying faculty members on a sliding scale based on the number of students in their courses. When the plan was presented to Steiner after several such discussions, he was emphatically opposed to this arrangement, suggesting instead that if funds allowed, remuneration should be increased equally for all. The decision was then made to give all the teachers a raise, although in fact the student fees for Steiner's lecture evenings covered the additional expense.[20]

For himself, therefore—and to the complete surprise of the school administration—Steiner had distanced himself from direct payment for his work.

When he first started teaching, Rudolf Steiner showed intense involvement and interest in the questions of his proletarian students, their life situations, and their desire for knowledge. In later presentations, he emphasized that in the course of industrialization—that is, in the process of performing mechanized work under capitalist conditions—members of the working class had awakened to their human dignity, so to speak, and forcibly developed "a consciousness of humanity." "In truth, consciousness of humanity awakened because of the machine and within the capitalist economic order." (328, 178)

> Because of their relationship to dehumanizing machinery and dehumanizing capital, proletarians had the opportunity to sense their consciousness turning toward the questions, "What am I as a human being?" and "What do I, as a human being, mean in the world?"
>
> I sincerely believe that our consideration of the social question will gain a new footing if we consider this: During the shift from the former merely instinctive view of human dignity and the individual's place in society to our modern, conscious conception of selfhood, the modern proletariat had a radical experience of being expelled from the old instincts into self-awareness, whereas most other people in different life contexts did not experience the shift as so radically revolutionary. (328, 15)

In lectures after World War I, Rudolf Steiner—who had not only studied the Socialist movement intensively but also witnessed it in part—pointed out repeatedly that until the Social Democratic Party's adoption of Marxism in the Erfurt Program of 1891, a (justified) central demand of the workers' movement under Ferdinand Lassalle had been the abolition of the wage relationship as a de facto debasement of the individual person:

> Instinctively, in their subconscious feelings, modern proletarians abhor the fact that they are forced to sell their labor power to employers in the same way that goods are sold on the open market. They find it repugnant that their labor is subject to the workings of supply and demand in the labor market just like a commodity. When we recognize abhorrence of "labor as commodity" as one of the basic impulses underlying the entire modern social movement, and when it becomes objectively apparent that even

Socialist theories fail to address this phenomenon radically and with sufficient urgency, then we will have found the starting point for approaching the burning issues related to the modern social movement. (328, 20)

Workers "abhorred" the fact that their labor power was understood as a commodity and issued what Steiner calls a "challenge to humanity" to search for ways of eliminating that commodity character. The bourgeoisie, however, took no interest in the actual situation of the working class, whose life was increasingly determined by material circumstances, leaving the workers who longed for insight and change to their own devices—and thus to the far-reaching consequences of the materialistic Marxist system of thought:

> The tragedy of the bourgeois view of life is that it failed to respond at the right point in time. In development of modern capitalism and democracy, the bourgeoisie missed what was needed. Essentially, the chaos we find ourselves in now comes not from below, from the proletariat, but from a misunderstanding of the times that rests squarely in the lap of the bourgeoisie. "It's my fault, all my fault" is what the leading circles ought to be saying to themselves. This sense of responsibility would engender a sense of what actually needs to happen. (330, 29)

In their longing for insight, proletarians sensed their consciousness "turning toward the questions, '*What am I as a human being?*' and '*What do I, as a human being, mean in the world?*'" The bourgeoisie failed to understand this phenomenon.[21] As a result, so Steiner tells us, the proletarian quest was abandoned to the effects and forces of materialistic thinking, which took hold of the working class with hypnotic power and reoriented it toward "purely economic processes" (23, 51). For working people, this materialistic thinking increasingly became the "foundation of their awareness of the nature of the human being" (23, 40). The working class and bourgeoisie of the late nineteenth century—responded to scientific materialism—"dead science," as Rudolf Steiner calls it (185, 50)—in very different ways. Steiner wrote:

> To the extent that major streams in world history can be called simultaneous, modern technology and modern capitalism developed simultaneously with modern science, which then won the confidence or faith of the modern proletariat. In their search for new and necessary conscious contents, the proletariat turned to science, relating to it differently in this respect than did the leading classes, who felt no need to make scientific viewpoints the psychological foundation of their view of life. (23, 39)

Members of the bourgeois class came to grips with materialistic views with "theoretical conviction" at best: "They felt no compulsion to relate to life on the feeling level in ways that completely coincided with materialistic thinking. Bourgeois sensibilities still contained vital but unnoticed remnants of a traditional faith in life" (23, 37f.). In contrast, the working class was unconditional in its approach to materialistic science:

> Working people took this science completely seriously and drew from it their own conclusions and consequences for life. The age of technology and capitalism affected them differently than it affected the members of the leading classes, whose lives were still ordered and shaped by soul-borne impulses. The leading classes had every interest in incorporating modern accomplishments into the existing fabric of their lives. Proletarian souls, however, had been torn out of that fabric, which failed to provide them with any sense of human worth in view of the contents of their lives. Proletarians sensed what being human means

through scientific thinking, the only thing that seemed to emerge from the old order of life with confidence-inspiring energy. (328, 11)[22]

Rudolf Steiner was certainly capable of honoring the life work of Karl Marx as an individual intellectual achievement: "I truly admire Karl Marx for his acute thinking, for his comprehensive view of history, for his great, all-encompassing feeling for the impulses of the modern proletariat, for his formidable critical insight into the self-destructive processes of modern capitalism, and for his many brilliant qualities" (330, 45). At the same time, however, Steiner was quite certain that as a dominant system of thought, materialistic Marxism would have disastrous consequences for both individual consciousness and the social order. In a written statement to this effect, Steiner quotes Goethe's words:

> An inadequate truth continues to work for a certain time, but in place of complete illumination a blinding falsehood suddenly sets in, which satisfies the world and beguiles centuries.

> Abstract terms and great arrogance are a sure route to unspeakable misfortune. (24, 35)

*

Rudolf Steiner's tenure at the Berlin Workers' School was during a time of spiritual upheaval, during years when it was becoming increasingly obvious that the workers' "challenge to humanity," as Steiner called it, was being distorted into purely economic demands. The Workers' School itself fell increasingly under the control of Socialist party politics:

> I was confronted with individual working class souls that slumbered and dreamed, and with a collective soul of sorts

that took hold of this portion of humanity, ensnaring its ideas, its judgment, and its attitudes.

We must not imagine, however, that these individual souls had died away. In this respect, I was able to look deeply into the souls of my students and of the working class as a whole. What I saw sustained me in the task I set myself throughout my activity there. At that time, the workers' position on Marxism was not yet what it would become twenty years later. They treated Marxism with due deliberation, like an economic Gospel, but later they seemed to become possessed by it, their proletarian consciousness filled with what looked like the effects of collective hypnosis (28, 378f.).

It seems to me that the proletarian movement would have developed very differently if a significant number of objective people had followed it with interest and if the proletariat had been treated with understanding. Instead, individuals were left to live their lives within the confines of their own social classes, and each class had only theoretical notions about the other. Wage negotiations took place when strikes or the like made them necessary, and all kinds of truly commendable welfare services were instituted. What was missing, however, was any attempt to consider these questions of world import in the larger spiritual context, which would have been the only way to eliminate the movement's destructive forces. At that time the "higher classes" were losing their sense of community, and egotism proliferated in ferocious competition. The worldwide catastrophe of the second decade of the twentieth century was already preparing to emerge. On the sidelines, the proletariat developed its own sense of community in the form of proletarian class consciousness. The working class participated in the "culture" developed by the "upper classes" only to the extent that it supplied them with material for justifying proletarian class consciousness. In the end, there was no bridge left between the different classes. (38, 379)

In 1904 alone, Rudolf Steiner gave ninety lectures in the Workers' School, but although his students repeatedly gave their non-socialist teacher their vote of confidence, the school's administration ultimately put an end to Steiner's teaching activity, which he had been able to continue for two and a half years after becoming general secretary of the Theosophical Society. "I can foresee that it will not work in the long run with people who insist on believing that materialistic ideas condense into bread" (39, 438; April 15, 1904). But by January 19, 1905, after his de facto exclusion from the school, he would have to write (in the above-cited letter to Marie von Sivers), "You know that I saw a mission in my activity in these circles. Here something has really been destroyed that I did not want to see destroyed" (262, 88).

In the preceding years, Rudolf Steiner had still thought that the materialism dominating prevailing dogmas might still be diverted to an idealistic track. In his history courses as well as in other contexts, he had identified the actual spiritual forces affecting the development of human society and culture. He took the (essentially existential) longing of his worker audiences seriously. With them, he discussed many issues and viewpoints that were both physical and metaphysical, opening up broad perspectives that had increasingly become the foundation of individual lives.[23] Basically, socialist materialism and its view of the human being had never really answered these working class questions. Instead, it paralyzed and exploited them, undermining them with ideology and creating a psychological situation with far-reaching consequences:

> Within the modern proletariat, any spiritual life that individuals approach through culture had been made to seem mere ideology. And because ideology cannot fill the human soul with enthusiasm or buoyancy or any awareness of

what it actually is in a higher sense, it leaves souls empty and dissatisfied. This psychological emptiness gave rise to the devastated mood of the proletarian worldview, which is one aspect of the real social question. As long as we do not realize that human beings must be cured of inclinations toward ideology, we will be unable to convey positive impulses to souls of the modern proletariat, which will remain filled with mere critiques of the recently developed technological and capitalist economic order and its worldview. (328, p. 59)

*

In this connection, Rudolf Steiner continued to see his teaching in the Berlin Workers' School as essential even after he joined the Theosophical Society. As early as 1903, he had written an article on "Theosophy and Socialism" for the Theosophical publication *Lucifer-Gnosis* and sent this issue—as well as earlier ones—to the school library, *"so they would be fully aware of his thinking."*[24] Steiner's two-part essay "The Social Question and Theosophy" was probably prompted not only by historical events in Russia, Steiner's experiences at the socialist Workers' School, and his familiarity with a large number of recent publications on solutions to the "social question" but also by G. L. Dankmar's extensive monograph, published in Leipzig in the summer of 1905, on the state of European culture in relation to the modern revival of occultism.[25]

In this comprehensive 626-page work, based on publications in "psychic studies" from 1902 to 1904, Dankmar (who was closely aligned with the "empirical spiritualism" of Karl du Prel) attempts to demonstrate the "cultural justification" of occultism."[26] In particular, Dankmar focuses on the ethical basis of socialism and the "socio-economic fulfillment of moral law."[27] Dankmar defines "occultism" in broad terms, e.g., "Occultism must become the science of far-flung ideas that have truth as

Die

kulturelle Lage Europas

beim Wiedererwachen

des modernen Okkultismus.

Geistige, soziale und politische Hauptströmungen

dargestellt von

G. L. Dankmar.

Motto: Ungläubige nun hört mich an!
Was ihr anbetet, bet' ich nicht an;
Was ich anbete, betet ihr nicht an:
Euerm Glauben seid ihr, ich meinem unterthan.
Koran: Sure 109.

Leipzig,
Druck und Verlag von Oswald Mutze.
1905.

their content and logic as their form."[28] He describes the development of occultism from the French Revolution to the end of the nineteenth century, focusing primarily on literary, philosophical, scientific, and economic viewpoints and tendencies.

Most of the book consists of fairly cursory treatments of the utopian socialism of Claude-Henri Saint-Simon, Auguste Compte, Louis Blanc, and François Fourier, along with discussions of Marx and Engels, but in his final chapter ("The Categorical Imperative of Occultism") Dankmar goes into detail on the contemporary social situation and the Theosophical movement, with reference to Rudolf Steiner's publications.

The last sixty pages of the book are devoted to an animated sketch of the real privations of the working class in an environment of liberalistic, egocentric individualism and a highly mechanized free-market economy that literally abuses and enslaves workers and their labor power. "It makes sense to talk about freely entering into wage agreements only if the parties are more or less equals. Today, however, employees are all too often forced to hire themselves out *at any price*. What use are rights if you cannot avail yourself of them?"[29] Dankmar defends the "social thinking" of ethical socialism: "The freedom and equal rights of the economically disadvantaged must be guaranteed in the same way as those of the economically powerful. The well-being of the individual must be the standard for the well-being of the whole. This is the *quintessence of social thinking.*" At the same time, however, Dankmar emphatically repudiates the political party that stood for this idea: "Socialism must not be confused with the much narrower concept of Social Democracy, which is a political party. As such, it is inherently pig-headed and one-sided, represented by weak and often uneducated or miseducated individuals."[30] He also emphasizes that the ethical socialist perspective, although it opposes established state churches, is aligned with the original precepts of Christianity:[31] "Christianity means helping the poor, not in the sense of alms, which have become insufficient, but in the sense of eliminating poverty as such. A single mighty breath of brotherliness and equality pervades the Gospels and the Prophets. As clear as crystal, Christ's teachings reveal the socialist ethical ideal of the solidarity of the human race."[32]

Dankmar emphasized the need for a future community ethic that would concretely permit the further development of individuals—especially in their economic and working life. "Industry exists to serve human beings, not vice versa. The *only* issue is whether the production of goods allows individuals to thrive."[33] In this context, Dankmar referred to the contribution of the theosophical movement and to Rudolf Steiner, whom he calls "brilliant."[34] Dankmar was familiar with Steiner's essays in *Lucifer-Gnosis* and quotes them repeatedly. He emphatically affirms theosophy's anthropological basis as well as its ideas about incarnation and destiny and its goal of a "brotherhood of humanity," but he sharply criticizes its tendency to turn away from acute social needs and toward the "beyond." In this context, he writes:

> We can only actively hope that the Theosophical Society, instead of providing murky allegories and a mythical terminology full of mystical and incomprehensible Sanskrit words, will take its principle of universal brotherhood seriously and throw itself into this brotherly activity to a greater extent. Theosophists should be less involved with eschatology because—as R. Steiner rightly observes—"their task lies in [this] life, not in the Beyond." It is essential for theosophy to flow into all our actions. We must live it.
>
> That said, we are fully justified in asking how theosophy relates to practical issues, to the economic circumstances of individual lives. It certainly makes sense that theosophy, with its fundamental principle of universal brotherhood, also ought to concern itself with socialism, which is based on the same principle. Rudolf Steiner says that "Theosophy must become the soul of social matters."

But he also charges—and rightly so—that the leaders of socialist efforts actually have no notion of socialist issues, and he finds it lamentable that at a time when the social question has become acute, the thinking of the masses is materialistic. This latter statement is certainly correct. We have already emphasized the perversity of shunting the train of socialism onto materialistic tracks, and we will return to it again. At the same time, however, Steiner admits that the machine and current industrial developments have created the proletariat's sorry situation (*Lucifer-Gnosis*, 1903, 6, p. 224). In other words, he acknowledges the impact of outer factors in the "karmically ordained environment" on individuals and on the masses. We are locked into real economic categories, and social and ethical activity must always go hand-in-hand. One is impracticable without the other. [...] Individuals living at the poverty level are both economically and culturally suppressed. Is the theosophical camp unaware that profound poverty is a source of immorality? [...] Above all, what we need is not sanctimonious theosophical talk but improvement in basic living conditions. [...] All theosophical ideas that do not adapt to existing economic conditions are mere worthless utopias. [...]

Steiner makes a carefully worded statement (*Lucifer-Gnosis*, 1903, 3, p. 115) to the effect that if the self-serving inertia of the bourgeoisie stands in the way of cultural progress, it will be superseded by higher ideals (although he does not say *which* ideals). Theosophy in general, however, is completely dismissive of (or at least indifferent to) practical issues. It even takes a certain pride in being unworldly. Died-in-the-wool theosophists are very reluctant to descend to earth from devachanic and karmic heights; they would sooner chew on ten Sanskrit words than inform themselves about the minimum basic pension. [...]

So far, unfortunately, theosophical activity has cloaked itself in Sanskrit and remained a mystery to most people. All too often, it has been the province of a spiritual aristocracy that enjoys the contemplative calm of a carefree existence and devotes itself to higher spiritual and psychological forms of recreation from that unworldly vantage point. As certain as it may be that occultism—as a pure phenomenon—cannot function on the ethical or cultural level without theosophy, it is equally certain that theosophy will become a significant factor in our culture *only if* it adapts to the real economic needs of its time. Let us hope that the theosophists will descend from their higher planes of existence to become pioneers of ethical progress on solid ground. May they place themselves in the practical service of humanity, and may their ethical striving focus on cultural activity! If theosophy descends from its icy isolation to consort with the common folk, if it truthfully and seriously places the ethical demand for universal brotherhood at the top of its program and acts accordingly without fear of the consequences, it will transform Christ's words "love thy neighbor" into social action and will become (and remain) the exquisite and inalienable property of all humanity.[35]

*

In a certain respect, Rudolf Steiner's social essays in *Lucifer-Gnosis*, which were published just a few months after Dankmar's monograph and referred to it both directly and indirectly, were a concrete response to its questions and omissions. Steiner agreed not only with Dankmar's criticism but also, for the most part, with the intentions he formulated for the future: "Social history is humanity's progress from the good to the better, and its ultimate goal is a community of individuals who want to be *free*, a community in which each one takes ownership of the other person's objectively justified aims.[36] With regard to society in its existing form and the future orientation of the spiritual science that he represented, Steiner wrote:

> For several reasons, [the spiritual-scientific movement] cannot show itself now in the face it will wear someday. One reason is that in order to first gain a foothold, it must address a particular group of people. [...] To the extent that suitable circumstances ensue, spiritual science will also find forms of expression that allow it to speak to other circles. (34, 220)

The "real fruit" of theosophical spiritual science, said Steiner, is by no means inner peace and private happiness for individuals. Rather, spiritual science—as a consistent means of training human thought and soul forces—makes it possible to *take up the tasks [of practical life] with insight and to seek ways and means of arriving at solutions"* (34, 193). Every social activity or reform requires real *"understanding of life"*—that is, well-founded judgment about life and its alignments, a "clear, objective view of the forces and powers at work in the world."[37] The "life teachings of spiritual science" result in a concrete training that successively enhances perception and cognition of the forces at work while simultaneously developing the moral will needed to intervene in the world in a healing way: "Working our way through spiritual-scientific ideas means enhancing our capacity for social action. In this connection, it is important not only which thoughts we take in through spiritual science, but *what we do with our thinking as a result* (34, 196).

Rudolf Steiner conceded that Dankmar was right in stating that the present state of the theosophical moment still revealed little of these developments and that in principle, therefore, all of Dankmar's expressed doubts and critiques were justified. Nonetheless, said Steiner, spiritual-scientific theosophy was only in "the early stages of its activity." *"As it continues to progress, it will introduce itself into all of life's practical aspects."*[38]

*

In *Lucifer-Gnosis*, Rudolf Steiner's description of "Theosophy and the Social Question," which led to the formulation of the fundamental social law, had been immediately preceded by long articles about the path of spiritual training—essays published years later in book form under the title *How to Know Higher Worlds*. Even in these essays, with their esoteric language and style of presentation (and especially in the last one, published shortly before his social essay), Rudolf Steiner had pointed out that achieving devotion and readiness to make sacrifices, along with loving and liberating one's "surroundings," were unconditional prerequisites to entering the higher, spirit world. There he wrote:

> Therefore, occultists of the white path cannot be expected to provide instructions for developing the personal, egotistical "I." They do not have the slightest interest in the individual's bliss. We may achieve that for ourselves, but white occultists are not charged with accelerating the process. They are simply concerned with the development and liberation of all beings, whether humans or the companions of humans. That is why they provide instruction only in how to develop the forces needed to participate in this work and why they place more importance on selfless devotion and readiness to make sacrifices than on all other qualities. (10, 214)

"*Ora et labora* was the Benedictine rule in the early development of Christianity. *Pray*—develop your being to comprehend the world spiritually—and *work*—apply your strengths in the service of others"[39] (Benediktus Hardorp).

In 1905, Rudolf Steiner held public lectures in the Berlin House of Architects on October 12 ("The World Situation: War, Peace, and the Science of Spirit"), October 26 ("The Social Question and Theosophy"), and November 23 ("Brotherliness and the Struggle for Existence"). In them, Steiner further developed these esoteric social perspectives in the light of contemporary challenges and in sharp contrast to prevailing social Darwinist paradigms.[40] In the same location, in a Christmas lecture given on December 14, 1905, a few months before his first presentations on a spiritual-scientifically based art of education, he said:

> What we intend to send out into the world is not just a dogma, not mere teachings or simply a philosophy, but *life*. Ideally, everything we say and teach, everything contained in our writings and our science, should make the transition into life, and it will do so when people practice spiritual science in all aspects of daily life. We will no longer need to talk about spiritual science when, without mentioning the term "theosophy" or "spiritual science," its life resounds in the words spoken to the faithful from all pulpits; when all courts consider human actions with a spiritual scientific sensibility; when all physicians approach and cure patients on the basis of spiritual science; when schoolteachers model spiritual science for growing children—in short, when spiritual science underlies everything thought, felt, and done on all our streets, then spiritual-scientific teachings will become superfluous. Our ideal will have been achieved; spiritual science will be an everyday matter. (54, 249f.)

*

2.

The Formulation of the Fundamental Social Law

Evolution is moving in the direction of totally uncompensated work. No one rejects the idea and no one can change it. Whereas Greek workers performed their work in bondage to their master and modern workers are compelled to work for pay, in the future all work will be performed freely. Work and income will be completely separated. That is the healthy state of social conditions in the future. You can see it already today.

— RUDOLF STEINER, BERLIN, OCTOBER 26, 1905 [41]

Organizing factories in the right way is already possible today.

— Rudolf Steiner, Berlin, October 26, 1905[42]

IN RUDOLF STEINER'S ESSAY "Theosophy and the Social Question," which appeared in late December 1905 and early February 1906 in issues 29 and 30 of *Lucifer-Gnosis,* he elaborated his views of the organization of labor and the economy, first presented in his lecture of October 26 in the House of Architects.

After some introductory remarks, Steiner began with a fundamental revision of the term "exploitation" as it had found its way into the social discussion through Marxist-Socialist theory. Although Steiner did not deny that contemporary living conditions produced concrete suffering, he placed value on seeing present circumstances as the "expression of an inner life" and social institutions as "creations of human souls" "that embody their perceptions, attitudes, and thoughts in these arrangements" (34, 205). In this connection, he emphasized that exploitation of human labor, although widespread, was not the result of deliberately harmful practices.

In his words, "On the large scale, no significant portion of humanity, no caste or class, is maliciously causing the suffering of any other portion. All claims to this effect are based on simple lack of insight. [...] Of course, those who exploit their fellow human beings would prefer that the victims of their exploitation did *not* have to suffer. We would make considerable progress if we could not only accept this as a matter of course but also adjust our perceptions and emotions accordingly" (34, 204). Seeing exploitation as the expression of a universally applied understanding of labor and remuneration rather than as essentially due to the moral perfidy of a particular class, said Steiner, marks the onset of cognitive activity based on a *"spiritual-scientific attitude"* toward *"social thinking."* He continued to elaborate:

> To a superficial view, it is easy to see individuals as oppressors if they own magnificent houses, can afford to travel by first class rail, and so on, or as oppressed if they wear cheap coats and have to travel fourth class. Nonetheless, using clear thinking to understand what I am about to tell you does not make you uncompassionate or reactionary or anything of the sort. Nobody is oppressed because I wear a certain kind of coat, but only because I pay too little to the worker who made it. *With respect to their fellow human beings*, an impoverished worker who pays little for his poor quality coat is in exactly the same situation as a rich man who has a tailor make him a better one. Whether I am poor or rich, I exploit others whenever I acquire goods without paying enough for them. Today, actually, we should never call anyone else an oppressor without first considering whether we are doing the same thing. Do you receive inadequate remuneration only for goods you sell to the wealthy? No, you also receive too little from your neighbors, who also complain about being oppressed, and yet acquire the products of your labor under exactly the same conditions as the wealthy people you both oppose. Just think this through logically, and you will discover alternative starting points for "social thinking" that are not the usual ones. If we pursue this train of thought, it will become obvious that we must completely separate the concepts "rich" and "exploiter." Today, being rich or poor may be due to our personal proficiency or that of our ancestors or to something completely

different. Exploiting the labor of others, however, has nothing to do with *these* things but a great deal to do with other things—specifically, with the fact that our institutions or the circumstances that surround us are entirely based on *personal self-interest*. We must think clearly here to avoid arriving at an incorrect view of the situation. Under existing circumstances, it seems only natural to acquire a new coat as inexpensively as possible, but if I do so, I have only *my own interest* in mind. That, however, is the perspective that governs our entire life. [...]

Introducing improvements to protect the working class will certainly do much to raise the standard of living for certain groups of people, but no matter how many such improvements we implement, they do nothing to mitigate the *essential character* of exploitation, which depends on *self-interest* as the basis for acquiring the products of other people's labor. If I apply whatever I have to satisfying my own self-interest, I *inevitably* exploit others. Even if I put protections in place to safeguard those people's labor, the change is illusory. If I pay a lot for others' labor, they will also have to pay a lot for mine, or improving their situation will worsen mine. (34, 205ff.)

In this essay, Rudolf Steiner developed the "functional concept of exploitation."[43] He took as his starting point the prevailing concept of labor as a commodity and emphasized the absolute necessity of a thorough reevaluation of related circumstances. According to Steiner, egotism is an actual force that shapes social contexts via the principle of direct compensation for human work: "our institutions or the circumstances that surround us are entirely based on *personal self-interest*" (34, 206). Under these circumstances, even seemingly socially exemplary arrangements and institutions (such as Robert Owen's model community in Indiana) that raise the living standards of individuals by demanding higher payment for their work, simply increase the intensity of

A notebook entry by Rudolf Steiner. 1905
Notebook No. 463. Rudolf Steiner Archive, Dornach

(ultimately) self-centered thinking and behavior. Rudolf Steiner's formulation stands in stark contrast to Adam Smith's principles of national economy:

> We assume that the totality of a human community can thrive best when individuals also reap the "full"—or at least the greatest possible—benefits of their work. But occultism based on deeper insight into human nature and the world teaches us the exact opposite, revealing all human misery as a simple consequence of egotism. At some point, misery, poverty, and need will inevitably arise in a human community that is based in any way on egotism. (34, 212)

In this essay, Rudolf Steiner developed his train of thought in simple and logically traceable ways, but his insights were actually based on original spiritual-scientific research. In this presentation directed toward the general public, Steiner did not discuss the basis of his statements but simply pointed out the need for a more extensive description of social interactions in terms of a theory based on "deeper, underlying" social forces—in other words, on theory that would be developed independently on the basis of spiritual science and then discussed in a scholarly context (34, 212).

At that time, however, in the late autumn of 1905—during the weeks of revolutionary upheaval in Russia and thus in a specific context of temporal forces—Steiner clearly chose to formulate an initial, sketchy response based on spiritual science and to simply "highlight" the *true laws of human collaboration.* His foundation in occultism allowed him to formulate his "fundamental social law" as the *"cosmic law of work"*:

The well-being of an entire group of individuals who work together is the greater, the less individuals claim the income resulting from their own accomplishments for themselves, that is, the more they contribute this income to their fellow workers and the more their own needs are met not through their own efforts but through the efforts of others.

By way of explanation, Steiner added:

> In the long run, misery and need will inevitably result somewhere from any institutions within a human collective that contradict this fundamental law, which applies to our social interactions with the same exclusivity and necessity that any natural law applies to natural consequences in its particular field.
>
> We must [...] not imagine that it is enough if we allow this law to stand as a general moral law or attempt to simply apply the attitude of working in the service of our fellow human beings. No, in reality this law functions as it should only when a collective of individuals succeeds in creating arrangements that do not permit individuals to claim the fruits of their own work for their personal use; if at all possible, all of those fruits should benefit the entire group. Each individual, in turn, must be sustained by the work of his or her fellow human beings. The crucial point, therefore, is that working for one's fellows and achieving a specific income must be kept completely separate. (34, 213)

According to Rudolf Steiner, concrete implementation of the paradigm he formulated at the turn of the year 1905/06 as the *"fundamental principle of social science and social activity"* (186, 46) would depend on individuals who were attempting "to find the way out of egotism." (34, 214) At the same time, however, he indicated that the egotism shaping our civilization could actually be overcome by organizing work appropriately: "In practice, [overcoming egotism] is totally impossible if the labor of individuals determines their measure of wellbeing or woe. It is inevitable that those who work *for their own sake* will eventually succumb to egotism. Only those who perform their work entirely for the benefit of others can gradually become unegotistical workers" (34, 14).

Thus Rudolf Steiner defined the turning point of our social future as a real issue of will, as the willingness of individuals to create new ways of working together and to found new social forms based on an anthropological concept of work—that is, on work as a selfless activity in support of the community's tasks. Once established, these social forms would then support their own further development. From the very beginning, Rudolf Steiner emphasized that under these changed circumstances, individuals would remain motivated to work only if they consciously experienced the reality of their common task—in other words, only if they are active (in full "I"-awareness) in the sphere where concrete common goals are set, and are capable of acting out of it on their own initiative and according to their individual aptitudes and strengths:

> Individuals who work for another person must see their reason and motivation for work in that person. Similarly, anyone who works for the totality must be able to sense the value, the essence, and the importance of that totality, which is possible only if the totality is something very different from a more or less indeterminate sum of individuals. It must be filled with a real spirit in which each individual can participate. Each one must be able to acknowledge the rightness of the whole and want it to be as it is. The totality must have a spiritual mission, and each individual must want to contribute to fulfilling that mission. [...] Right into the details, the spirit of the totality must be alive. (34, 215f.)

*

In this connection, Rudolf Steiner described the importance of theosophical spiritual science as a force that overcomes egotism, a transformative, ideal/spiritual force for receptivity in all human soul faculties. "The only help will come from a spiritual worldview inherently capable of coming alive in human thoughts, feelings, and will—in short, in the entire soul of the individual" (34, 216). On the basis of theosophical spiritual science, individuals sense themselves as beings incarnated into space and time with specific gifts and tasks, as irreplaceable members of humanity. In the motivational space of this experience of self, individuals can access not only the intentions that drive their lives but also a connection to their surroundings. Steiner tells us that through active self-realization in and together with their surroundings, individuals can lead the ongoing process of creation further. From the very beginning, Rudolf Steiner's theosophical lectures and publications had emphasized that the contents of theosophy as a specific worldview were not its only essential aspect; even more important were the training opportunities these contents offered individual souls. Although Rudolf Steiner did not expressly say so in his essay, he clearly saw the theosophical movement as an organ for implementing social tasks, as a pioneering group of individuals whose spiritual training and advancement allowed them to actually tackle these tasks on behalf of civilization— hopes echoed in Dankmar's constructive criticism: "Let us hope that the theosophists will descend from their higher planes of existence to become pioneers of ethical progress on solid ground. May they place themselves in the practical service of humanity, and may their ethical striving focus on cultural activity!" Similar opportunities to model the reshaping of labor and the economy clearly existed among limited groups of people as early as 1905, as Steiner briefly sketches in his essay:

> Already now [...] certain human communities are developing the potential for something of this sort. They will make it possible for humanity to accomplish—with their help—a sudden leap forward in social evolution. Although such human communities are known to occultism, its task cannot be to speak publicly about such things. (34, 218)

At the same time, however, Rudolf Steiner's essay also emphasized the universal applicability of the *"cosmic law of work"* as he formulated it, its transcendence of individual human communities brought together by destiny, and the universally available opportunities for its practical implementation on either the large or small scale. Steiner wrote:

> Wherever this law makes its appearance, wherever individuals work in its spirit to the extent possible in their position in human society, the effects—even if only slight in any individual case—are always positive. Overall social healing and progress will be pieced together entirely out of such individual effects. We can each work in the spirit of this law in our own fields. Nowhere in the world is there any position in society, whether seemingly insignificant or ever so influential, that would prevent such activity on the part of an individual. (34, 218)

Steiner emphasized that although unconditional implementation of the fundamental social law was not yet possible under existing circumstances in 1905, tendencies in that direction were indeed already possible. In his lecture in the Berlin House of Architects on October 26, he said: *"Organizing factories in the right way is already possible today."*[44] He left no doubt that the evolutionary tendency he outlined there would be part of the future:

> Evolution is moving in the direction of totally uncompensated work. No one rejects the idea and no one can change it. Whereas Greek workers performed their work in bondage to their master and modern workers are compelled to work for pay, in the future all work will be performed freely. Work and income will be completely separated.
> That is the healthy state of social conditions in the future. You can already see it today. Work will be performed freely,

out of insight into the need for it. People will work because they look at other people and recognize that those people need their work. In antiquity, work was the payment of a toll or tribute, performed because it had to be performed. Now it is based on self-interest and on the compulsion that egotism exerts on us. Because we want to survive, we want to be paid for our work. We work for our own sake when we work for payment, but in the future we will work for the sake of our fellow human beings, because they need the work we can do. Through our completely voluntary activity, we will clothe our fellow human beings and provide them with everything else they need. Income must be completely separated from work. In the past, work was a tribute; in the future, it will be a free-will offering that has nothing to do with self-interest or recompense. When I allow my work to be dictated by consumption, by what humanity needs, I enter into a free working relationship and my work is an offering to humanity. Out of love for humanity, I contribute work according to my strengths, making them available to humankind.

This must be possible and it is indeed possible, but only when sustenance is separated from work. That will happen in the future. Then, no one will own the product of their own work anymore. Humanity must be taught to work with no thought of compensation, one for all and all for one.[45]

*

At the end of his two-part essay, Rudolf Steiner announced: *"More details will be presented soon"* (34, 221). The planned continuation of his study, however, never appeared in *Lucifer-Gnosis*. Many years later, Rudolf Steiner reported that he had refrained from publishing additional practical details (both immediately and in all subsequent years until the end of World

War I) because of lack of response to his *"initial treatise"* (185a, 213). *"At that point I stopped because no one paid any attention"* (338, 30). In particular, it seems, there was no response from people who could have created model facilities to implement Steiner's guidelines on a larger practical scale, although Steiner himself was convinced of the feasibility: *"Today it is already possible to organize factories in the right way."* The few attempts within the Theosophical movement were clearly quite paltry:

> It proved possible to give detailed advice in some instances, but again, the circumstances proved inadequate and the right consequences failed to materialize. (186, 235)[46]

The same fate lay in store for Rudolf Steiner's practical perspectives on education, which he began presenting in lectures in the spring of 1906, followed by a more extensive written work (*The Education of the Child in the Light of Spiritual Science*). To Steiner, there seemed to be a real possibility of establishing schools based on spiritual science, schools with radiating effects that would reshape civilization: "Today's lecture deals with things that can be implemented immediately" (55, 133). But again, nothing of the sort happened at that time:

> My little book *The Education of the Child in the Light of Spiritual Science*," which appeared right at the beginning of the anthroposophical movement, was already available and included all kinds of suggestions. In fact, it already contained a whole system of education, but it was not generally received as anything more than tips on childrearing for mothers. There were repeated questions about whether a particular child ought to wear blue or red or have a yellow or red bedspread or what that child should eat, and so on. These efforts were all well and good, but not especially far-reaching. (310, 173)

Understandably, given the theosophical movement's failure to take up what Dankmar called its "cultural task," the general public continued to view the spiritual science Rudolf Steiner represented *"as some sort of religious sectarianism on the part of a few strange fanatics"* (34, 344). As a consequence, valuable years were wasted.

*

3.

The Threefold Social Organism (1919)

I am not envisaging that revolutionary events will occur overnight but simply that all individual measures in public and private life will have to line up in a single direction if the social body is to be healed. [...]

[...] It is not simply a matter of choosing to either implement or disregard some program but of recognizing something that wants to become a reality. We must make it a reality because it is inherent in the historical growth forces that we will need in the present and near future.

— RUDOLF STEINER, BERLIN, FEBRUARY 5, 1919

(328, 42FF.)

What is really needed today is a straight path from ethics, religion, and spirituality to the most mundane social issues of national economy.

— Rudolf Steiner, (188, 238)

T HE YEAR 1917 is an epochal year in modern history, the year when today's global configuration clearly begins to appear. In the east, the Soviets come to power through the February and October revolutions in Russia. In the west, the US becomes a crucial power by entering the war. Both Lenin, the Soviet leader, and Wilson, the US president, develop propaganda campaigns for their war goals: socialism, liberation for the masses, and democracy are slogans that conceal other impulses. By contrast, the Central Powers (Germany and the double monarchy of Austria-Hungary) do not formulate idealistic concepts to appeal to all individuals and ethnic groups but limit their war goals to annexations of territory in the west and east.

In this situation, Count Otto Lerchenfeld of the Bavarian state parliament questions Rudolf Steiner about what to do. In response to Count Lerchenfeld—and later also to Count Ludwig Polzer-Hoditz—Rudolf Steiner develops the idea of the threefold social organism, designed to dismantle the centralized state and lead to cultural autonomy, a national government limited to legal matters, and a cooperative economy. These ideas are then presented to leading politicians (including the German foreign minister

and the Austrian prime minister) as potential war goals
for Central Europe—that is, as German drafts to be used
especially in negotiations with the East. Numerous efforts
to make them a reality, however, meet with no success.
A second major attempt to make the ideas of threefoldness fruitful for social activity is not launched until 1919,
under very different circumstances.[47]

*

During the World War I, Rudolf Steiner spoke about the
causes and background of the war, calling it a "terrible catastrophe...that partially exposes the social riddle in its original
form" (188, 212). *"The catastrophic war is like the final act.*
Human impulses have run out, and what they leave behind will
require a new understanding" (328, 178). In his lectures at the
Berlin Workers' School, Rudolf Steiner had already pointed
to the intrinsically fateful dependence of intellectual and cultural affairs on economic forces and constellations. This forced
dependence had developed over the course of the nineteenth
century as a result of radical encroachments by the economy as
it transformed Marxist materialistic theory into a (secondarily
constructed) reality.[48] "Because economic activity has grown
beyond not only our politico-legal system but also our cultural
activity, it has swamped everything, so to speak, with hypnotic
effects on human thoughts, perceptions, and passions" (332a,
23). In later years, Rudolf Steiner also saw the encroachment
and dissociation of intrinsically different spheres of activity as
one of the primary causes of the war. In 1919 he wrote:

> A temporal phenomenon that has developed in recent cen-
> turies—namely, the dependence of cultural and political
> activity on the economy—is seen as natural and inevitable.
> We do not notice the truth of the matter, which is that
> this dependence has driven humanity into the [present]

catastrophe [...]. (24, 18f.)

Governments and economies are not developed by the same forces. The chaos of recent times is due to attempts to transform nations into economic associations. (23, 16)

Repeatedly and in detail, Rudolf Steiner described economic interests and conflicts as the primary driving forces within the nexus of forces that caused the war: *"economic factors, economic elements [...], that have made use of state powers"* (328, 71).

If [these economic forces] had been left to develop purely on the basis of economic activity and their own interactions, they would never have been able to lead to this catastrophe. They have done so because a bogus political body allowed them to utilize the state's political forces, which sent armies into the field on their behalf. (328, 71)

In Berlin in late May of 1917, Rudolf Steiner was asked by Count Otto Lerchenfeld to draft ideals for a new social order for Germany that would also serve as conditions of a future peace treaty. In that conversation with Lerchenfeld, Steiner's perspectives on the threefold social body emerged for the first time. Lerchenfeld describes the meeting in his diary: "Spent three hours today at Dr. Steiner's. The solution to everything now stands before me. I know that no one else can provide it. He called it the threefolding of the social body, and its effect on me was like the egg that allowed Columbus to imagine the world as round."[49] Two years later, Rudolf Steiner formulated it like this:

The habitual ways of thinking that we owe to current political circumstances include a firm belief in the "impracticability" of changing these circumstances. However, any measures this habitual thinking attempts to preserve or initiate will be destroyed or left behind by historical developments. As the catastrophe of the World War has revealed, the essential needs of modern humanity cannot possibly be met through further amalgamation of the cultural, political, and economic realms. Economic and intellectual/cultural conflicts that assumed the form of national enmities have necessarily produced outcomes that would be impossible if, on the international level, cultural affairs dealt only with cultural affairs and economic interests with other economic interests. (24, 26)

Freedom is the fundamental principle in cultural matters, which must be based on the freedom of individuals to apply their unique capabilities. Equality is the fundamental impulse of the governmental and legal system, where everything must emerge from awareness of equal human rights. Brotherliness, which will develop through associations, is what must prevail on the grand scale in life's economic aspect. (330, 39)

During the war years, Rudolf Steiner barely mentioned the subject of social threefolding in lectures, although he brought it up in conversations — with leading politicians, among others — as a "Central European program," and with regard to foreign policy concerns.[50] In Dornach during the first few days and weeks after the end of the war and the beginning of the revolution in Germany, he explained his ideas with particular emphasis on economic aspects, as in his "fundamental social law." One year earlier, in November 1917, he had begun speaking in Dornach about the "problem of evil" in all its destructiveness and egotistical antisociality as an issue for contemporary civilization (and thus also contemporary consciousness) to resolve.[51] In late October 1918, continuing on this theme, he once again—for the first time in many years—referred back to statements he made in Berlin in the late fall and winter of 1905:

In the context of society, it is disastrous when individuals are paid for their work and beneficial when their livelihood comes not from their own work but from other sources in society. This statement seems to contradict what I just said, but the contradiction is only an apparent one. Not being paid for work will make work valuable. We must aim—rationally, of course, not in any Bolshevistic way—to divorce individuals' work from their means of subsistence. [...] When people are not paid for their labor, money loses its power over work. The only remedy for the current abuse of mere money is to structure society so that individuals cannot be paid for their work but their ability to acquire essential goods is ensured through other means. In that case, of course, people could not be forced to work because they need money [...] In future, we will not be allowed to equate money with human labor but only with lifeless goods. In exchange for money, we will receive only lifeless goods, not human labor. My dear friends, this is a tremendously important point. (186, 49)

Steiner tells us that as long as money is understood and used as payment for labor, it actually functions as a destructive "instrument of power" (186, 53). This is especially true when money takes the form of inherited capital that earns dividends and exploits human labor: "Ahrimanic power is active in money that appears to be produced by money. You cannot inherit money without receiving a certain amount of Ahrimanic energy along with it" (Ibid.).[52] In this way, the "socially active inner human being" (24, 72) is literally weakened, distorted, and prevented from unfolding (as it is in other respects by "overprivileged government").

In his postwar lectures on the urgent need to restructure society on the basis of "insight into the social body's fundamental forces" (23, 91), Rudolf Steiner frequently read from a lecture he had given in Vienna in the spring of 1914:

A spiritual view of social life reveals that terrible potentials for spiritual cancers are beginning to develop. For anyone with a penetrating view of life, this terrible and oppressive sight arouses great concern for our culture. Even if we could suppress everything else that makes us enthusiastic about spiritual science, the sight of these growing potentials would leave us screaming for world healing. If the social body continues on its current path of development, the result will be cultural damage equivalent to malignant tumors in the natural human body. (328, 182f.)

For Rudolf Steiner, "real insight into the nature of the social body" (328, 24) and the resulting division of that body into three autonomous, separately administered areas—along with implicit limitations on the economy's sphere of influence— were not only a future possibility conceived by spiritual science but an absolute imperative for our time and civilization: *"I believe that the thoughts I am expressing are not those of an individual but rather an expression of the unconscious will of European humanity"* (24, 12.) Hans Georg Schweppenhäuser calls social threefolding a "fundamental structural law."[53] As such, it is one of essentials that will "allow modern humanity to survive" (24, 113). In a magazine editorial, Rudolf Steiner wrote: "Healing our civilization will not be possible unless we become fully conscious of the intentions of our time, which lie hidden in a dense thicket of impractical, illusionary party stereotypes" (24, 13).

*

In 1919, Rudolf Steiner included his "main social law" or the "fundamental social law of human work" (328, 89) in various presentations on threefolding, explaining the law's contents anew and referring to his efforts of fourteen years earlier. In Zurich on February 12, 1919, for example, he said:

At the beginning of this century, I already attempted to draw attention to this fundamental law in an essay on the social question that I wrote as editor of the magazine *Lucifer-Gnosis*. At that time, however, I was preaching to deaf ears, and unfortunately that is still the case in this area today. According to this law, inasmuch as individuals are part of the social order, they do not really work for their own benefit. Note this well: inasmuch as people are part of the social organism, they do not work for their own benefit. Any work we perform can never redound to our benefit, not even in the form of actual income, but can only be done for the benefit of other people. Similarly, what other people do must benefit us. The active principle here is an actual social law, not simply an ethical call for altruism. Just as we cannot redirect our blood into channels not determined by the body's circulatory system, we can do nothing to change the fact that our activity benefits everyone else and everyone else's activity benefits us.

Of course this statement sounds paradoxical, but if you investigate the actual circulation of human work in the social organization, you will discover that work leaves the individual who performs it and then benefits others; what each person receives is the product of other people's labor. As I said, paradoxical as it may sound, it is true. In the social order, we cannot live off our own labor any more than we can nourish ourselves by consuming ourselves. (328, 89f.)

This understanding of the "fundamental social law of human labor" played a significant role in defining and shaping the economic aspects of Steiner's concept of threefold society. As Steiner had already indicated in 1905, if we really reflect on the nature of human work, it becomes obvious that labor cannot be viewed and recompensed as if it were a commodity. Although labor clearly affects the economic realm of the production, distribution, and consumption of goods, it is a human quality with an inherent social function, and as such does not belong to the economy. In line with Steiner's statements and suggestions of 1905, one of the key features of his conception of threefolding in 1919 was the elimination of the commodification and marketing of human labor. According to Steiner, only threefolding the social body would be able to effectively "liberate" human labor from exploitative commodification:

> The point here is that human labor cannot be compared in price to a commodity of any sort. The labor of human beings is something very different from manufactured goods, and as such it must be removed from the economy. That will happen only when economic activity is seen as one limb of the social organization, separate from government or the politico-legal system. (330, 20)

> We cannot strip human labor of its commodity character unless we find a way to extract it from economic processes. Our efforts cannot be directed toward transforming the economy so that human labor can assume its rightful place *within* it. Rather, our question must be how to extract labor from the economy so it can then be molded by social forces that will strip it of its commodity character. (23, 54)

> Any thinking person ought to be focused on the economic question most important to the happiness or misfortune of the civilized world, yet we completely fail to notice this question, namely: How can manufactured goods—commodities—be dissociated from labor so that labor can no longer be considered a commodity? This goal is achievable. Non-human goods and human labor can be objectively dissociated by making adjustments in the direction of the threefolding I have described to you. (186, 234)

Attempted revolutions in Russia and Germany that focused on economic restructuring still clung to the (supposed) commodity character of human labor: "This line of sight will never discover how to put an end to labor as a commodity. A restructured economy will simply have other ways of making labor a commodity" (23, 54f.). Rudolf Steiner, however, tells us that the threefolding of the social order would make it possible to assign labor to the sphere of human rights, where it truly belongs: "The right to work is also a human right" (331, 167). The economy always tends to "absorb" labor and misuse it as a commodity: "Economic activity cannot help but transform everything that comes within its reach into a commodity" (338, 80). Because of this tendency, one of the functions of a democratically elected government is to protect labor and preserve its true significance: "The legal system must always assign labor to its natural, altruistic place" (328, 90).

Furthermore, says Steiner, the functions of independent cultural activity include recognizing the true character and anthropological significance of human labor and encouraging adaptation of its motives to the ideal. In this way, Steiner tells us, our cultural and political systems must repeatedly infuse the economy with forces that "realign developing antisocial tendencies with society" (24, 74). In other words, when economic dominance threatens to destroy the social order, the other two systems must correct and even heal it.[54] They "counteract the constant damage caused by the economy even as it occurs" (24, 101).

With regard to the "social structuring of human work" (24, 128), Rudolf Steiner describes in practical terms how the extent, type, and time of work would be determined in the threefold social order on a politico-legal basis *before* workers enter into the economic process (333, 21). In other words, work itself is not a part of any commodity or service contract in the economic realm. Instead, it belongs to the autonomous domain of human rights. Of actual economic contracts, Steiner said:

> No matter what kind words we may say about them, any economic contracts that are wage agreements will always result in dissatisfaction on the workers' part. A humane existence for all parties will emerge only when no more labor contracts are negotiated and when contracts cover only production, which depends on the work of both managers and laborers. Only then will workers feel like they are freely part of the process in relation to managers. (333, 21)

In explaining the economic aspects of threefold society, Rudolf Steiner always emphasized that individual initiative remains needed and must be further developed, especially in the entrepreneurial realm: "The social organism must be based on the free initiative of individual capabilities and on the free understanding of what they can accomplish. There is no other way" (189, 134f.). He predicted that the anti-individualist and collectivist economic and social efforts of the Russian Revolution would inevitably lead to economic disaster: "Eliminating individual intellectual and spiritual capacities would also destroy the economy. Establishing a world bureaucracy—the Leninist and Trotskyite ideal—is out of the question. It would most certainly eliminate independent intellectual initiatives and cause the starvation of the social organism" (190, 43). "Replacing individual initiative with abstract collectivism would mean the extinction or death of the economy, as Eastern Europe will prove if it remains under its current leadership much longer. For the well-being of the human community, individual spiritual initiatives must flow into the movement of the means of production. If we deprive individuals of these initiatives, the result is the extinction or death of the economy" (332a, 48). In the context of social threefoldness, however, the relationship between employers and manual laborers (or between "managers" and "workers") must be strictly a legal relationship, not one of selling or purchasing labor, and as such it has consequences for agreeing on adequate "wages" and understanding the nature of "earnings":

In reality, the relationship is this: The so-called wage laborer works together with the head of the enterprise, and what takes place between them is really a discussion about how to distribute the proceeds. This discussion, however, is [usually] concealed behind all sorts of deceptive circumstances—power dynamics, and so on. To put it paradoxically, we might say that wages do not exist even today; there is only distribution of proceeds, although as a rule the economically weaker party gets shortchanged. That is all there is to it. The point here is to avoid imposing the consequences of society's error on reality. As soon as the social structure I described in my book *The Social Future* is in place, it will become obvious that "employees" and "employers" work together; their titles cease to be meaningful and the relationship becomes one of distribution of proceeds. When this happens, the wage relationship completely loses its significance. (332a, 73f.)

*

"Managers" and workers in a company work together on a "joint production," a "common product." In principle, according to Steiner, all those involved in any way in the making of the product—including its concrete financial and administrative contexts—should be fully involved in and informed about its progress:

> Regular opportunities for employer and employees to discuss the state of the business must be considered a necessity, as important as the machine work itself, so the employees always have an overview of the current situation and goals for the future. The employer must always be ready to tell the employees everything in detail so the factory is embedded in this shared thinking. This is essential. It is the only way to develop a relationship in which workers can acknowledge that the employer is as necessary as they

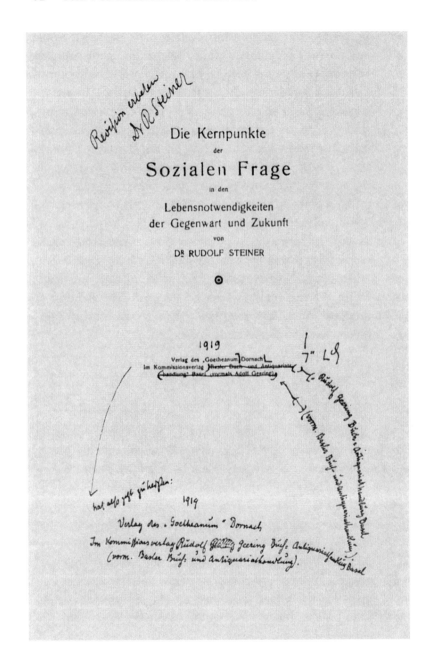

Rudolf Steiner: title page of *The Social Future.* 1919

themselves are, for without the employer, what would their work mean in the context of society? The employer's function is to ensure that they are working in the right place. (189, 134)

Rudolf Steiner saw both knowledge of the entire production process and a concrete understanding of society's need for the product as essential elements of a future motivational view of work. The basis of this new attitude toward work is no longer individuals' egotistical interest in being paid but rather their selfless acknowledgement of the needs of the community (or totality). As Steiner noted in a fundamental spiritual lecture in Dornach on November 12, 1916, increasingly specialized division of labor in the future economy will no longer allow blue-collar workers to have any direct connection to what they produce because their part in it will be so small. In earlier times, workers were involved in the entire production process, but now they are becoming ever more removed from the final product as the world of work becomes increasingly "objectified" and largely independent of individuals. The world of work is no longer an extension of the workers' hands, and achieving any emotional connection to it is becoming increasingly difficult.[55] In his threefolding lectures after the end of World War I, Rudolf Steiner repeatedly emphasized both the shadow aspect of this process *and* the opportunities it presented. For example, in Zurich on October 26, 1919, speaking about how work will be motivated in the future, he said:

> The old devotion to and direct connection with the object produced no longer exist, but they must be replaced by something else. Human nature cannot tolerate the absence of an incentive to work such as that formerly provided by the immediate pleasure of producing an object. What can replace that incentive? It can be replaced only if human horizons expand, only if individuals are called upon to

develop real human interest in all the people in their larger circle—and ultimately, in everyone belonging to the same social organism. No one needs to feel limited by circumstances, not even the man off in some corner whose function in the larger context is only to turn a single screw. The feelings he has developed for others must accompany him into his workplace and go with him when he leaves. He needs a living view of his connection to human society; he needs to know that if it is no longer possible to work for the immediate pleasure of producing something, he can certainly still work because he feels himself to be a valuable member of his human circle. (332a, 93)

Eleven years earlier, in a lecture at the Berlin House of Architects in March 1908, Rudolf Steiner said with similar emphasis:

Think about what individuals can do when they work out of love for other people. Love for the product of work is unnecessary; what is needed now is a bond between people. You cannot bring back love for the product, because that was bound up with primitive, simple conditions. The future, however, must bring a great, all-encompassing understanding and love from person to person. We will be unable to develop real impulses for future development or human salvation until individuals find the motivation for their activity in the deepest impulses of love for their fellow human beings.

According to Steiner, the increasing division of labor in modern economy calls for intrinsic altruism in individual activity: "In purely economic terms, egotism is impossible. As the division of labor increases, we can no longer work for our own benefit; everything we do must be done for the sake of others" (340, 46). "Whether we like it or not, egotistical work is an economic impossibility in a social organism based on the division of labor. All the results of an individual's work must accrue to the totality"[56] (329, 170f). Furthermore, questioning the egocentric payment motivation for work (or even eliminating it in the context of social threefolding) gives rise to the possibility—and even the necessity—of a higher, broader motive for individual work. Rudolf Steiner tells us that if *"working for others means working out of social need"* (340, 48), future economic processes depend on employees developing not only a comprehensive understanding of production and of the factory as an economic unit with a "common spiritual life," but also a real experience of their "connection to human society" and its needs in terms of production and consumption:

> Egotism is based on need or consumption. If we approach this fact with the necessary understanding, we will not ask how egotism can be overcome in the economy but rather how altruism can satisfy our legitimate egotism. This second question sounds less idealistic, but in fact it is the real question. (332a, 191)

> Once again, a time must come when every detail of life becomes interesting. The interest we once devoted to objects will have to be applied to how the details of work are integrated into the social structure of humanity. Where we formerly looked at the products of labor, we will then look at the people who need those products. In the past, we loved the products, but in the developed souls of the future, human love and brotherliness will emerge so individuals will be able to know why they work where they do. (83, 248)

In the future, according to Steiner, the needs of individuals and society will necessarily remain characterized by egotism, but each individual's consumption of life's necessities will be served by increasingly altruistic, "love-imbued" production—not the self-serving, profit-oriented production in the tradition of private capital or the market economy, but production that is oriented toward meeting real needs. As Rudolf Steiner explained in detail in his presentations on social threefolding, the economic sphere of the threefold social order will be administered by concrete "associations" of consumers and producers. The economy will be responsible for the availability, circulation, and adequate pricing of goods, and an "objective public spiritedness" (340, 152) or "brotherliness" (333, 29), will allow it to develop on the basis of perceived economic needs:[57]

> Today here is no shortage of people telling us that our economy will become good when people become good — therefore, you people have to become good! Such judgments, however, actually make as little sense as the somewhat more extreme statement that if my mother-in-law had four wheels and a steering wheel front, she would be a bus. There is just as little connection between the assumption and the conclusion.
>
> *The Social Future* is not based on moralizing, which would not be out of place elsewhere, but rather on the fact that the economy itself should demonstrate the need for selflessness in the flow of economic factors. (340, 153)

In his essay from the winter of 1905-06, Rudolf Steiner had already discussed the "facilities" that would need to be created to allow the "fundamental social law"—understood as the "main social law of human work"—to take effect. In 1919, his descriptions of associative organizations expanded on earlier perspectives, and after World War I they also began to become a reality in concrete "ways of organizing daily life"[58] (23, 140). As expounded by Rudolf Steiner in numerous lectures and written works in 1919, the "threefolding of the social order" was a bold, far-sighted plan, especially with its view of a peaceful world order in the age of the rapidly developing world economy.[59] Nonetheless, in many different contexts Rudolf Steiner left no doubt that social threefolding as he presented it was an immediate challenge, something conceived for and attempting to manifest in a very specifically defined historical time:

> "This is not a question of establishing a thousand-year kingdom. It is something the spiritual world is attempting to implement for a short period of time." (192, 16)

> "[The threefolding of the social organization] is something the spirit of our present time is demanding of people and wants to see realized—in fact, is attempting to manifest. The chaos we are experiencing now is due to the fact that human thinking (and human actions, especially) are at odds with how the spirit of the time is thinking and acting. (192, 18)

> Threefolding is necessary because our times demand it. Later—not now, but three or four centuries from now—a time will come when threefoldness will have to be overcome, and people will have to think about how to undo it. This reality is in stark contrast to millennial thinking, such as the idea of a thousand-year kingdom, a state of blessedness that (once established) will allow humanity to remain in that state forever. In the real world, however, things are not that convenient—they are always right for specific places and times. (192, 389)[60]

As formulated by Rudolf Steiner, implementing the threefold social order was primarily a task for Central Europe: "I believe the thoughts I am expressing are not those of an individual. Rather, they express the unconscious will of *European* humanity." They were also time-specific, emerging as they did at the end of the World War that began in central Europe and at the

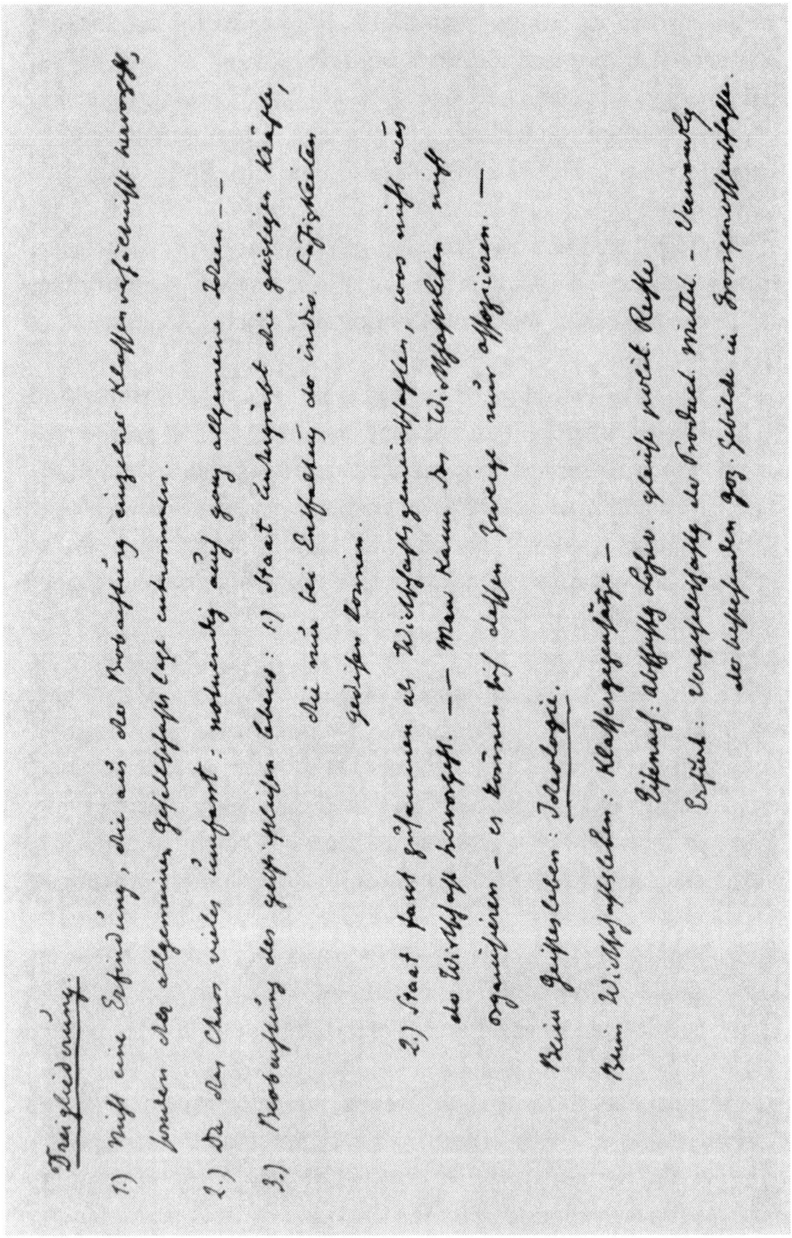

Dreigliederung.

1.) Nicht eine Erfindung, die aus der Beobachtung einzelner Klassenverhältnisse hervorgeht, sondern der allgemeinen Gesellschaftslage entnommen.

2.) Da das Chaos vieles umfasst: notwendig auf ganz allgemeine Ideen – –

3.) Beobachtung des geistig-geschichtlichen Lebens: 1.) Staat untergräbt die geistigen Kräfte, die nur bei Entfaltung der indiv. Fähigkeiten gedeihen können.

2.) Staat fasst zusammen als Wirtschaftsgemeinschaften, was nicht aus der Wirtschaft hervorgeht. – – Man kann das Wirtschaftsleben nicht organisieren – es können sich dessen Zweige nur assoziieren. —

Beim Geistesleben: Ideologie.

Beim Wirtschaftsleben: Klassengegensätze –

Eisenach: Abschaffung Lohnv. gleiche polit. Rechte

Erfurt: Vergesellschaftung der Product. Mittel. – Umwandlung der bestehenden soz. Gebilde in Grossgenossenschaften.

Ita Wegman Archive, Arlesheim

beginning of the era that would be characterized—in Steiner's words—by *"Western imperialist politico-economic ambitions"* (192, 121) and the corresponding worldwide development of Anglo-American military and economic power.[61] In the East, said Steiner, this era would be characterized by a fundamentalist uprising—a development that certainly became evident at the latest by the last third of the twentieth century. As an initiate, Steiner attempted to suggest guidelines and ways of working that would shape an alternative future: "Today, anything that does not originate in initiation is no longer useful in developing social thinking" (197, 38). He was trying to introduce the public to *"socially effective ideas from beyond the threshold of physical consciousness"*—ideas that were accessible to rational thinking and that if taken up and implemented in a timely fashion would pave the way for actual, positive future developments in human civilization.[62] Steiner's book *Towards Social Renewal* appeared in the spring of 1919; in some instances, reviews in the press were exceptionally positive.[63] Its publication was followed by Rudolf Steiner's personal commitment in an "elucidation from below" (185a, 123) and—initially—lively interest on the part of the general public and large segments of the working class.[64] In spite of all this, however, the threefolding movement was ultimately unable to achieve any noteworthy degree of recognition.[65] *"Misunderstood [...] on all sides"* (83, 278), Rudolf Steiner encountered serious ideological resistance from political parties and unions "amidst the destructive absence of ideas" (24, 148) and experienced an intensified recapitulation of his experience at the Berlin Workers' School. In a letter written in late June 1919, after two-and-a-half months of effort on behalf of social threefolding in Württemberg, Rudolf Steiner wrote:

> No doubt we would make great progress among the proletariat if the party leaders were not so aggressive in pulling the carpet out from under us. The proletariat is more obedient to them than Catholics ever were to the heads of their

church. And the bourgeois masses are sleeping like babies, roused only by—or to make—"declarations," and are the puppets of manipulators whose only effective methods are those opposed to spirit...[66]

(Not coincidentally, this letter was to Johanna Mücke, who had been a convinced Socialist and had been working in the office of the Liebknecht School during Steiner's tenure there, and later worked with Marie von Sivers to develop the Philosophisch-Anthroposophischer Verlag to publish Rudolf Steiner's works.)

Even within the Anthroposophical Society, Rudolf Steiner's best efforts encountered countless instances of resistance as he tried to help people understand his social initiatives—and to free them from the Society's self-centered attitudes. The Anthroposophical Society, although no longer as upper middle class or reclusive in character as the earlier Theosophical Society, was certainly not functioning on the level of Steiner's work. "People who come together in the movement we call anthroposophically oriented spiritual science ought to feel like a nucleus that radiates forces for social renewal. Attempts at social change that come from other directions can be very useful, but they still need work: Real social change can come only from spiritual impulses. *That is why we would have expected the best understanding of these conditions to arise in circles that are part of this movement*" (193, 121; italics added). On September 14, 1919, in Berlin, Steiner said that only those "with a finger on the pulse of the times" can be anthroposophists "in the truest sense of the word" (193, 158) and that being a real anthroposophist requires an attitude of active involvement and willingness to realistically confront the forces and powers of the times, including their destructive dynamics.[67]

As early as February 1, 1919—weeks *before* the beginning of the threefolding movement—Rudolf Steiner, responding to problematic social attitudes in Dornach and in line with the position he had articulated in Berlin a decade and a half earlier, said:

> In modern life, we have materialistic capitalism on the one hand and on the other hand something just as bad, namely, the attitude, "Oh, what do I care about Ahriman! Let Ahriman be Ahriman; I am busy devoting myself to my soul's inmost impulses and to the spiritual world. I am concerned with soul matters and seek the spiritual world as it can be found within. What do I care about the Ahrimanic nature of credit, money, fortune, and ownership? What do I care about the difference between annuities and dividends, gross income and net earnings, and so on? The business that concerns me is the business of my own soul!"

But just as a human being unites body, soul, and spirit between birth and death, so too outer physical existence unites the impulses we can discover in the inmost structures of the human soul and the impulses at work out there in the economy. The blame for the recent catastrophe falls equally on materialistic capitalists with their particular ways of thinking and on those others who want to remain exclusively godly and spiritual-scientific. They impose abstract limits on spiritual science to serve their own purposes and refuse to intervene in everyday reality enough to imbue it with thinking.

This is what has moved me repeatedly to tell you that you should not take this anthroposophical spiritual movement simply as an opportunity to hear Sunday afternoon sermons that do your souls good because they talk about eternal life, etcetera. The point is to adopt this anthroposophical movement as a means of tackling the burning issues of modern existence in truly meaningful and appropriate ways. And one of the first things we need to do is to understand where to begin [...] (188, 231f).

Rudolf Steiner also took exception to the carefully articulated assumption that the "fundamental social law" and the "three-folding of the social body"—along with their particular concept of work and fellowship—were ahead of their time (or ahead of the state of human moral development), and therefore could not become a reality at present. Steiner stated emphatically:

> Today we often hear, "Well, these ideas are all very well and good and it's nice to imagine them being implemented, but people simply aren't ready for that. The masses are not mature enough." But what does it mean if we say the masses are not ready? We think differently about these people if we recognize the relationship between ideas and reality and if we see through the reality of practical affairs. We know that deep inside, if they choose to go there, enough people are now capable of completely understanding the issue. Usually, what holds us back is only lack of courage. We lack the energy to push through in the way we could if we were able to develop complete self-awareness.[68] (332a, 203f)

4.

The Individual and the Community

*"When two or three are gathered together in my name,
I am there among them."*

— (MT. 18:20)

Although the outer words that describe threefoldness
may not seem to refer to Christianity, in fact the threefolding of the social body is intended in the sense of
real, true, practical Christianity.

— RUDOLF STEINER (334, 192)

Resistance [to threefolding of the social body] will crumble in the face of the goal that *humanity as a whole* will have to establish ever more consciously on the basis of the necessities of modern life.

— Rudolf Steiner, 1919 (23, 142[69])

THE FUNDAMENTAL SOCIAL LAW and the threefolding of the social body were the measures Rudolf Steiner proposed to counteract tendencies dominating the early twentieth century. Developed in an age of machines, technology, and rampant economic egotism, these countermeasures were an attempt to identify the conditions and guidelines needed for developing a future peaceful social order. They bucked the prevailing trend, which Rudolf Steiner repeatedly described as inevitably leading not only to the destruction of natural resources and the means of livelihood for future generations but also to the disruption of all human connections.[70] In a lecture in Dornach during World War I, on November 12, 1916, he said:

Purely outward advances in the development of work would lead to the dissolution of all ties within humanity. People would become increasingly unable to understand each other or to develop relationships that satisfy the requirements of human nature. Individuals would increasingly pass each other by, safeguarding only their own interests, and would be incapable of relating to each other except as competitors. This must not be allowed to happen, or the human race will fall into complete decadence. [...]

> It would be hell if the human race were controlled entirely
> by competition and addiction to acquisition.[71] (172, 94)

Rudolf Steiner's critique of civilization, however, was never moralistic in character. He knew all too well that the culture of enhanced personality in the industrial age was (and is) no tragic accident of creation but rather a temporary necessity in the development of the human "I." Experiencing the world through science has recently allowed people to detach themselves from their surroundings as distinct personalities, in contrast to the secure tradition of community that had persisted for millennia. In modern times, it became both possible and necessary for individuals to extricate themselves from old social ties.[72] People "took their chances with their own personalities" (186, 164), responding to an anthropological need to develop the capacity for individual freedom. The "primal phenomenon of [modern] social science" is how Steiner described the force of antipathy and egotism—or even actual "antisocialness" (186, 175)—that is present even in the dimension of the higher senses. He also emphasized, however, that our task is to penetrate these present and future tendencies with insight and to overcome them:

> Our era is intended to make human beings realize that they
> are egotistical beings by nature. To overcome egotism, we
> must first investigate all of its sources in human nature.
> (186, 209)

When Rudolf Steiner spoke in Bern on December 12, 1918, his remarks were emphatically future-oriented:

> Today humanity has no inkling of how strong antisocial
> urges will become between now and the third millennium,
> but for human beings to evolve correctly, these antisocial
> urges must continue to develop.

In earlier times, the development of antisocial urges was not the spiritual bread of life that fed humanity's evolution, so no countermeasures were needed. In modern times, antisocial urges must be developed in order to cultivate the individual Self. Like it or not, human beings are subject to this evolution. But now the time has come to introduce social forms to counteract this evolutionary tendency. Inwardly, antisocial urges must be active so human evolution can reach its peak; outwardly, however, society must be structured to prevent human beings from losing their connections to each other in this life. What society asks of us now is nothing more than to provide the necessary counterbalance to the prevailing tendency in humanity's inner evolution.

*

In the early twentieth century, Rudolf Steiner's fundamental social law emphasized the anthropological dimension of working for others as an antidote to potentially destructive forces: "We cannot allow the impulse to work to be based on egotism. It must arise out of a view of the totality" (56, 248). Even in his earliest lectures on the subject, Steiner spoke of "social sensitivity to one's surroundings" as a prerequisite to any future-worthy work arrangements.[73] He also said that "brotherly love for other people" (186, 312) and the interests and needs of "the other" (as representative of the entire community) can become the actual motivation for work. *"Fundamental law: the individual can only work 'for others,'"* Steiner wrote in his notebook in 1919 (328, 86). In his lectures on social science during the Vienna East-West convention three years later, in June 1922, he said:

Most of all, however, our times are suffering from the lack of any basic social understanding of how work can be incorporated into the social organization correctly, so that everything we do is truly performed for the sake of our fellow human beings. We can acquire this understanding only by learning to really insert our "I" into the human community. New social forms will not be provided by nature but can emerge only from the human "I," through real, person-to-person understanding—that is, when the needs of others become a matter of direct experience for us. (83, 245)

Steiner tells us that the human impulse to work must be anchored in the "I," in each person's individuality. "If human beings ... are to remain human, the incentive to work must be present in each one" (198, 184). Ultimately, this also means in the individual in his or her immediate social context. In a certain respect, the work of each individual "belongs" to humanity (185, 213). According to Steiner, the individual "owes" the community his or her individual contribution and input— whether physical or mental—to the success and preservation of the whole:

> "The individual cannot want anything of what he or she produces; individuals owe their work to the social community. Conversely, each individual must live entirely from what the social community provides. (266/1, 129)

Rudolf Steiner explained this "fundamental law of human work" again in greater detail immediately after the end of the war's destructive dynamics. Speaking in Dornach on November 30, 1918, he elaborated:

> We have no interest in our fellow human beings if we believe we can be sustained by money we have inherited or acquired through any means other than work, which is the normal way to acquire money today. No one can

live on money alone. We must all eat, and what we eat must be produced by human beings. We need clothes, and everything we wear must be produced by human beings. Human beings spend hours working so I can have a coat or trousers to wear. Those people work for me. What sustains me is their work, not my money. My money has value only inasmuch as it gives me the power to take advantage of work done by others. Under today's social circumstances, we begin to be interested in our fellow human beings only when we see, in spirit, that x number of people must work for y number of hours to sustain us in this social context. Making ourselves feel good by saying, "I love my fellow human beings" is not the point. We do not love human beings if we believe that money is what sustains us, yet meanwhile we have no notion at all of the people who work on our behalf to meet our basic needs.

But the thought that x number of people work to provide our basic needs is inseparable from another thought, namely, that we must repay society—not in money, but in work—for the work done on our behalf. We are interested in our fellow human beings only when we feel responsible for paying back, in one way or another, the amount of work performed for us. [...] Interest of this sort, which is the prerequisite of a healthy social order, begins when we start to feel indebted to the society in which we live. (186, 46f.)

In his presentations on threefolding in subsequent years, Rudolf Steiner spoke repeatedly of the need for *"interest in the structure of society"* or *"real social interest"* (186, 47) as essential to the future of human civilization. At the same time, he also spoke of a fundamental interest in other people, in the concrete circumstances of their lives and in their accomplishments on behalf of the community: "Interest in the other person is what is needed. Formerly instinctive, it must now be acquired very consciously. The main nerve in society is each person's interest in the other." (186, 167) Steiner tells us that positive evolution is possible only through work based on such interest, work that is non-egotistical at heart and takes place in the context of *perceived* needs and tasks, in intrinsic "devotion to the whole" and in "love for the human social order":[74]

> As I have said in various contexts, understanding society is primarily a question of understanding individuals and developing individually differentiated interest in them. Wanting to get to know and understand human beings must become our most important task for the future. (186, 24)

*

Ultimately, an individual's work is his or her individual assignment in human life, and as such it must also be seen in the greater context of the person's biography and social history. When questioned by workers in the Liebknecht School in Berlin, Rudolf Steiner answered that happiness is not the prime motivator in human life; individuals have specific assignments on earth, and accomplishing those tasks gives meaning to individuals' biographies while also integrating them into the context of society. And in the spring of 1905, in a lecture in the Berlin House of Architects, Steiner said:

> As long as individuals seek only to satisfy their needs, they are personalities. When they do anything that transcends these efforts, they are individualities. The source for such actions can be found only in each individual.... This is where people acquire specific character, where they imbue their mission with something unique. (53, 311)

Seven years later, in February 1912, Rudolf Steiner pointed out that the social convention most hostile to a real understanding of human incarnation and reincarnation was "the principle that we must receive payment corresponding to the work we do"[75] (135, 87f.). In the same lecture, Steiner describes the positive impact of the idea of reincarnation and karma:

> Becoming convinced of reincarnation and karma and discovering ways of bringing that idea into daily life will transform our life as we move into the future. It will create totally new ways of living and a totally new human community. (135, 85)

Beginning with his earliest spiritual-scientific presentations on work in the context of society, Rudolf Steiner had emphasized that theosophy or anthroposophy—understood as the spiritual study of the human being and the world—was essential to humanity's further evolution, especially in terms of work and its place in a future social order. The path of spiritual-scientific training is a way of enhancing and sensitizing our capacity to be interested and participate in the destiny of individuals and of the world; ultimately, it paves the way for a "culture of insightful selflessness."[76] Steiner's spiritual-scientific findings provided a new basis for understanding the human being. They offered a means of fundamentally updating what it means to be human—the "image of the human being" in its anthropological, social, and cosmic connections, which had been almost completely supplanted during the development of materialistic science and culture:

> Today human beings know little about human beings. Spiritual science is only at the beginning of its cosmic assessment of human dignity and human nature. In real life, people today know little about human beings. As a rule, we do not penetrate deeply into the soul-essence of our fellows. A more profound social system, however, will require a new understanding the human being, and this new understanding will have to become a factor in human evolution. (193, 18f)

The guidance of anthroposophical spiritual science paves the way for the development of concrete organs for perceiving not only the situation of other people and of the community—in short, "social understanding"—but also the destined task of one's own incarnation and life's work. In Stuttgart on June 29, 1919, Rudolf Steiner explained:

> The most radical thought that must take root in modern humanity is this: We must see our physical existence not only as preparation for life after death but also as the continuation of a spiritual life before birth. This understanding will transform us from lazy people who would rather do nothing to individuals aware of having a mission to complete on earth. Until people are imbued with this idea, they will inevitably sink into materialism. (192, 251)

Understood in this way, every person on earth has an individual "mission" to complete successfully in connection with other people—a process intrinsically related (although not completely equivalent) to the person's actual work. To work for others, whether physically or spiritually, in the sense of the fundamental social law is one of the individual's most fateful tasks.[77] Shortage of work is one of the most tragic aberrations of modern times: "Unemployment! People can't find work, but the work must exist because the people are there.

In a healthy society, work that is not getting done cannot be superfluous; its absence *must* be felt somewhere. So much unemployment, so much work not getting done" (36, 33). In the associative organizations of the threefold social order, individuals become self-actualizing by acting in concert, pooling their individual capabilities and possibilities: "The central event here is the individual expressing his or her own being out of interest in others." Rudolf Steiner's pupil Georg von Arnim explains further:

In the broadest sense, seeking motivation for all our work in other human beings and seeing the essence of that work as the connection it establishes to our surroundings are both expressions of the human individuality, which is carried by destiny and in turn shapes destiny.[78]

Rudolf Steiner tells us that individuals bring their own destiny-borne impulses for life and work (and thus also their own unique capabilities and possibilities) into earthly existence as part of their independent spiritual life: "Everything individual in us is basically an aftereffect of life before birth" (191, 178). In contrast, brotherliness that develops within the economic process on earth is a seed or nucleus for the future: "Everything developed in our interactions with each other on earth is the seed of life after death. [...] The social element sows the seeds for life after death" (191, 187f.). Against this background, the "social understanding" we experience in the economic sphere is the prerequisite to our future evolution; through others, we awaken more profoundly to our own individuality and its destiny:

> We are living in an epoch that highlights the need for social understanding. We will be reborn in an epoch of understanding the destiny of individuals. When we speak today of the need for social understanding, we do so not out of any merely abstract impulse but in connection with earthly humanity's innermost evolution. (191, 179)

It is only from the earthly perspective that economic activity (the sphere of human work—the production, distribution, and consumption of goods in its material dependence on what Rudolf Steiner calls the "subhuman" realm) appears to be the "lowest" level of human existence. Accepted and understood for what it is, it harbors the beginnings of higher spiritual development in the future—an "esoteric" aspect of threefolding related to the temporal threefold structure of human existence. Rudolf Steiner discussed this aspect in a number of lectures. In Zurich on February 11, 1919, speaking on the future-oriented character of society's economic aspect, he said:

> Something is developing that forces us human beings down into the subhuman realm, so to speak, but we are reprieved by the fact that what develops through brotherliness in economic life stays with us and accompanies us when we pass through the portal of death into the supersensible world. Just as earthly spiritual life points to its origin, reflecting our supersensible spiritual life before birth, our economic activity and what develops in us under its influence—social interest, a feeling for human community, brotherliness— point to supersensible life after death. (193, 53f.)

*

Paving the way for "healing in the structure of human society" (186, 167) was the defining intention for Rudolf Steiner in all his suggestions for shaping the society of the future Even in Steiner's early formulations of the fundamental social law, "well-being" and "healing" were formative concepts: "The *well-being* of a community of individuals working together is the greater, the less individuals claim the income from their own production for themselves."

These terms also appear repeatedly in his later presentations and explanations: "In the social context, *healing* results only when individuals secure their livelihood not through their work, but from other sources in society"[79] (186, 49). Rudolf Steiner rephrased this idea as the "motto of social ethics" for his exemplary co-worker Edith Maryon, inscribing it in her copy of his book *Ausführung der Dreigliederung des sozialen Organismus* [Essays concerning the threefold division of the social organism]:

The healthy social life is found
When in the mirror of each human being
the whole community finds its reflection
And when in the community
The virtue of each one is living. (40, 298)

Elsewhere, Rudolf Steiner points out that in configuring the society of the future, the real issue will not be overcoming human individualism but rather "discovering" community in the "I" (83, 246). Real, "healing" brotherliness is a mercurial, Raphaelic impulse.[80] It consists in "one individual's social participation in everything another person experiences outwardly and inwardly" (328,124), i.e., in actively finding one's way into the other person's essential core and situation in life, as the foundation for a new, "I"-based social community imbued with selflessness.[81] The Christological substance of the associated participatory processes (with regard both to each concrete Other and the Community as a whole) was described by Rudolf Steiner in a meditative mantra in a course shortly before the beginning of World War I:

As long as *you* feel pain
That passes me by,
The Christ works unrecognized
In the being of worlds,
For weak is the spirit
That can feel suffering
Only in its own body.[82]

In the Matthew Gospel, we read Christ's words, "Anything you did for one of my brothers here, however humble, you did for me" (Mt. 25:40). In Düsseldorf on June 15, 1915, eight months after his course for wartime "samaritans" (medics), Rudolf Steiner elaborated, "Those who acknowledge other human beings as their brothers will be recognized by Christ as *his* brothers" (159, 318).

Rudolf Steiner: Modeled clay, head of Christ. 1915

*

Although Rudolf Steiner gave only a few explicit indications on this subject (primarily to members of the Anthroposophical Society), it is not difficult to see the Christological—or Christocentric—thrust of even his earliest attempts at social reform. *"To make the Christ Impulse a reality and to do what Christ wills for our time"* (186, 185) was clearly the guiding principle behind his activity in word, print, and deed. Above and beyond all modern efforts to make "the Christ" a reality in human actions (189, 49), Steiner repeatedly emphasized that the Christ *"must enter humanity as a social impulse"* (189, 47). If the social structure is "humanity's body" (187, 196), all efforts to heal this body—especially in the economic sphere of brotherliness—are paths toward (and prerequisites to) the future working of Christ.

Steiner's anthroposophy as a whole was more than just a Christ-centered doctrine. He understood it as Christ's means of speaking and revealing himself under early twentieth century conditions: "We take anthroposophically oriented spiritual science in the right way if we do not believe that the content of Christianity is exhausted in the Gospels. We know that Christ is truly there always, until the end of earthly time, not simply as a dead force to be believed in, but as a living force that repeatedly reveals itself anew. And what is he revealing at present? The content of modern anthroposophically oriented spiritual science, which not only speaks of Christ but is intended to express what the Christ wants to say, in the form of human thoughts, to human beings now" (193, 17). Rudolf Steiner tells us that at present, it can and must be possible to ask questions of the Christ-Being and to receive answers, albeit beyond the threshold of physical consciousness. In this sense, the fundamental social law and the threefolding of the social body were undoubtedly included in the contents of "Christ's new speaking" (193, 60). At present, according to Steiner, the Christ can be heard speaking *"in the language of practical life"* (197, 186). On February 11, 1919, Rudolf Steiner said in Zurich:

> Although of course we should read the Gospels over and over again, that is not all we should want to do. We should also hear what [the living Christ] has to reveal to us through his ongoing presence among us. In our time, this is what he reveals: Change your ways (in the words of his forerunner John the Baptist). Change the thinking that opens up to you the vision of your threefold humanity, which is demanding a threefold division of the forms in which you spend your earthly existence. (193, 55)

Three months later, in June 1919 in Heidenheim in Württemberg, he said:

> What is now being announced in the program of the "threefolding of the social body" is the Christianity of today—spiritual revelations clad in outer forms. This is what human beings need, the only real basis or possibility for changing our thinking and relearning what humanity so urgently needs. (193, 100f.)

In his anthroposophical lectures, Rudolf Steiner indicated repeatedly that present and future social developments could demonstrate a real connection to Christ and that the "mysteries" of future community are to be understood in the sense of Christ's words, *"For where two or three have met together in my name, I am there among them"* (Mt. 18:20). In Steiner's words:

> In a certain sense, ever since the event of the Mystery of Golgotha in the earth's evolution, everything related to human community belongs to the Christ-Impulse. The essential point here is that the Christ-Impulse belongs not to individuals but to the human community. Understood

as Christ Jesus himself intended, it is a great mistake to believe that individuals can relate to the Christ directly. Christ lived, died, and was resurrected for humankind, for humanity as a whole. (193, 48)

By incarnating into the earthly body of Jesus of Nazareth at the turning of the millennium and by undergoing death on Golgotha, the Christ-Being sacrificed himself for the sake of the fate of humanity and the earth. He united himself with earthly destinies. We must see Rudolf Steiner's emphasis on a future understanding of work as sacrifice in the context of these spiritual-social processes: *"Then we do not work for the sake of our own existence; the work we do is an absolute sacrifice for humanity"* (93a, 231). The intention Steiner formulated in the context of social three-folding, "to replace present systems of government worldwide with organizations imbued with brotherliness" (185, 223), and thus to make a Christian "socialism" possible, is based on the ability of individuals to identify selflessly with the being and circumstances of their counterparts as well as with the needs of the whole, "so that individuals feel unhappy if not all are as happy as they themselves are, or if their individual happiness is purchased at the expense of depriving others" (140, 56). Rudolf Steiner tells us in these future economic and social forms, the Christ-Impulse will be active in the direct devotion of individuals and in "kindling brotherhood." *"To the extent that we sense the need for brotherliness, we imbue ourselves with Christ"* (187, p. 50).

*

In Stuttgart on November 22, 1920, Rudolf Steiner spoke about economic associations in the threefold social body:

Associations are the living embodiment of brotherhood. Just as the life spirit is meant to live in the sphere of rights, so too, through imbuing economic activity with the Christ, the earliest potential for the spirit human lives in associations. These possibilities are not provided by the earth. We human beings can achieve them only by imbuing ourselves with Christ, who is now approaching and appearing to us in etheric form. (197, 203)

Imbuing ourselves "with Christ, who is now approaching and appearing in etheric form," says Steiner, will enable us to create a Christ-imbued, associative economy as an active organ of the "spirit human." Since 1910, Steiner's lectures on the etheric reappearance of Christ had occasionally mentioned its inherent moral and social dimension.[83] The creation of a threefold social order consisting of an independent cultural realm, a brotherly economy, and a democratic sphere of rights was—and remains—connected to this event. In one lecture, Steiner described the reappearance of Christ as "intimately related" to understanding threefolding (197, 163). The economic sphere of brotherliness—in which we are actively involved in meeting the needs of others—clearly belongs to the sphere of the forces of empathy, of shared joy and pain: *Other people's needs [must] become a matter of direct experience for us, so that our "I" actively lives in the "I" of others.*[84] In May of 1912, Rudolf Steiner described this process as actively shaping Christ's etheric "garments"[85] :

> Whenever a feeling of shared joy or pain develops in a human soul, it exerts a power of attraction for the Christ-Impulse. The Christ unites with the human soul through compassion and love, which are the forces out of which the Christ will shape his ether body until the end of the Earth phase of evolution. (143, 183f.)

> For when I was hungry, you gave me food; when thirsty, you gave me drink; when I was a stranger you took me into you home; when naked you clothed me. (Mt. 25:35-36)

The Christological background sketched here informs all of Rudolf Steiner's explanations of the fundamental social law, the threefold social body, and the development of a "society of peace" for humanity (54, 53)—a new civilization, international in its orientation, that feels responsibly united with the totality of cosmic events with regard to humanity's future and the life and fate of the other natural kingdoms. Rudolf Steiner calls this "humanity's goal of community" (23, 144). In 1929, four years after Rudolf Steiner's death, Steiner's colleague Dr. Ita Wegman took up the subject of human responsibility for the future of the earth and the plant and animal kingdoms in an essay on the "Mystery of the Earth" (in the Christian and Pauline sense). "For the created universe waits with eager expectation for God's sons to be revealed. It was made the victim of frustration, not by its own choice, but because of him who made it so, yet always there was hope" (Rom. 8:19-20). With great foresight, Wegman's wrote:

> Along with technology, the modern era brought human dominion over natural forces, and as a result human beings have become responsible for part of the natural world. It will not take long before we see this responsibility grow further.
>
> Initially separated, natural and historical processes increasingly merge. In ancient times, this was so only in isolated instances. The magnificent Renaissance city of Venice stands in the sea on pilings made from trees that once forested the mountains of Dalmatia. The climate change that resulted from this deforestation is one small example of larger instances to come.
>
> This new relationship to nature also applies to the human being as such. As educators and physicians, we confront a bit of nature in what we see as heredity, and increasingly our job will be to transform it consciously. If humanity neglects this process, it will soon confront natural phenomena that it has brought about without recognizing its

own involvement. Phenomena will emerge that defy explanation. Nature, which until now has seemed to be governed
by eternal laws, will seem to fall into chaos. This world
situation now lies in the very near future. Nature is beginning to reflect the chaotic behavior of human beings, as evi-
denced by catastrophes and aberrations. We human beings
see them in nature's mirror without recognizing our own
reflection.[86]

*

Even in his earliest spiritual-scientific publications and lectures,
Rudolf Steiner pointed out that the central task and mission of
theosophy—with its spiritual understanding of human beings and
the cosmos—was to become the "soul" of a future world community. Steiner repeatedly emphasized that spiritual science was a
community-building force that could unite individuals in the core
of their being in a higher association that would transcend all
boundaries of gender, nationality, and religion. To Rudolf Steiner,
theosophical (and later, anthroposophical) spiritual science was
both evidence and a real manifestation of a "free spiritual life"
that will help human beings not only achieve a meaningful and
socially effective view of life but also shape that vision into a
reality, with consequences extending into the creation of a brotherly economic sphere: "Of itself, an independent spiritual life will
necessarily develop social understanding, which in turn will give
rise to very different types of stimuli than those provided by the
hope of economic gain" (23, 108). Through these social stimuli,
modern spiritual science will develop humanity's capacity for
peace as Christ intended: "You, O Christ, have spoken to those
who walked with you: *I am at peace in the world; this peace
can also be with you, because I give it to you*" (343, 471). In
1919, looking back on the example of the construction of the
Goetheanum in Dornach and its social dimension during the war
years in central Europe, Rudolf Steiner said:

Basically, during all those years of war, what type of place was the [Goetheanum]? Throughout the war, people from all nations always worked together there with no less understanding than earlier, whether their discussions were necessary or not. The understanding that emerged from a shared spiritual view has already become a reality there, if only within that small circle. We have performed an experiment in this field, so to speak. We have been able to demonstrate that people who are willing to make the effort can understand each other. (332a, 119)

A real "community spirit," said Steiner, was active in the "small circle" of those working in Dornach during the war. In future, to the extent that the necessary conscious prerequisites and general living conditions can be brought about, this spirit will also be able to work in a "shared community" that is based on selflessness and international in scope. The *polis* of antiquity and the *city* of medieval times implemented seminal social processes and structures in a geographically limited space; but, according to Rudolf Steiner, developments after the end of the nineteenth century point toward an actual "world community" based on both full achievement of individualization and free and voluntary socialization, i.e., on the concrete experience of "community spirit."

In a society based on force, the will of the individual worked within the whole. Conversely, in the shared community of the future, a common will must become active in the individual.

But how will that be possible? A common will can only arise out of the interaction of individual wills such that individuals are able to feel free within the collective rather than subjected to a democratic tyranny. What does this require of the collective will? Individual souls, individual human spirits, must be able to feel at home in and in agreement with the common will. This means that the spirit and soul active in each individual must live in the collective will of the community. This is possible only if those shaping the collective will are able to take the individual will into their own willing, feeling, and thinking in complete understanding of the individual human being. What the individual senses as personal spirit, soul, and body must flow into the will of the whole. That is what the common will must contain.

It was different in instinctive power-based societies, where individuals were accepted by the whole because they did not assert their own will within that whole. It was also different in the barter society, where individual will had an impact and a coincidental community of sorts emerged. But something very different is required if an organized will of the whole is to work on the individual. It is unacceptable for anyone involved in shaping the will of the whole to fail to understand real human nature. A view of life based on abstract natural science that focuses only on outer nature and can never understand the whole human being is not acceptable. We will have to approach life through a spiritual science that encompasses the whole human being—body, soul, and spirit—and that can therefore also call forth understanding of the individual on the level of feeling and willing. (332a, 170f.)

Throughout his life, Rudolf Steiner actively applied his anthroposophical spiritual science to efforts in this direction with his anthroposophical spiritual science. In 1905/06, during the period of initial success after he was forced to give up his work at the Berlin Workers' School, Steiner formulated the fundamental social law and explained it as follows:

If someone is supposed to work for the whole, he or she must sense and feel the value, the essence, and the importance of that whole. This is possible only if the whole is something very different from a more or less indefinite sum of individuals. It must be filled with a real spirit in which everyone participates. Each one must be able to acknowledge that the whole is good and right, and as he or she wants it to be. The whole must have a spiritual mission, and each individual must want to contribute to fulfilling that mission.

This spirit of the whole must be alive and working, right down into each individual. (34, 24)

Ultimately, however, this "spirit of the whole must also be understood as the "Christ Spirit" and "representative of humanity"—"Not I, but the Christ in me," as Paul puts it—who can be present in all individuals and unite them with the community—that is, with their actual fellow human beings and the totality that supports them. The experience of this totality belongs to the "I" and becomes the source of social activity:

Inasmuch as [individuals] carry Christ in themselves, the "I" of humanity lives in them; to that extent, they *are* humanity.

The healthy social life is found
when in the mirror of each human being
the whole community finds its reflection.
And when in the community
the virtue of each one is living.

(40, 298)

Notes

1   Works by Rudolf Steiner cited in the text and notes are listed as (Gesamtausgabe volume, page number).
2   Cf. Götz W. Werner: *Ein Grund für die Zukunft–das Grundeinkommen*. Third edition, Stuttgart 2006.
3   Cf. Thomas S. Kuhn: *Die Struktur wissenschaftlicher Revolutionen*, Frankfurt 1967; Ludwig Fleck: *Entstehung und Entwicklung einer wissenschaftlichen Tatsache. Einführung in die Lehre vom Denkstil und Denkkollectiv*. Second edition, Frankfurt 1980; Gerhard Kienle: "Die Bedeutung der Anthroposophie für die Neugestaltung des Universitätslebens" (1982) in: Peter Selg, ed.: *Gerhard Kienle. Leben und Werk*, vol. 2. Dornach 2003, pp. 371-382.
4   In a different lecture, Rudolf Steiner said, "If you think about it, it was not so very long ago that independent institutions of higher learning were absorbed by the state. Universities used to be independent entities, each with its own standing and reputation. They were autonomous corporate bodies. Now this autonomy is completely lost, and they have become the loyal servants of the state in all aspects. In contrast, the 'head' of the social system—the economy—has become hypertrophied. All thinking begins with economics, and replacing the standpoint of throne and altar with the standpoint of offices and machines does not bode well for making the social organism viable" (190, 40).
5   Cf. Peter Selg: *Die Kultur der Selbstlosigkeit. Rudolf Steiner, das Fünfte Evangelium und das Zeitalter der Extreme*. Dornach 2006.
6   Cf. Werner: op. cit; Werner: *Wirtschaft – das Füreinander-Leisten*. Karlsruhe 2004; and Georg Vobruba: *Entkoppelung von Arbeit und Einkommen. Das Grundeinkommen in der Arbeitsgesellschaft*. Wiesbaden 2006.

7   Dieter Brüll: *Der anthroposophische Sozialimpulse – ein Versuch seiner Erfassung.* Schaffhausen 1984, p. 282.

8   In my opinion, Brüll's review and assessment of Rudolf Steiner's intentions (see previous note) remains unsurpassed. See in particular pp. 117ff. and 237ff. on how Steiner's perspectives have been partially or completely reinterpreted (or insufficient implemented) in anthroposophical settings.

9   As early as 1920, Rudolf Steiner said, "Humanity today runs the risk [...] of loss of soul and spirit. [...] We live in a time when human beings face the risk of losing their souls due to the materialistic impulse. This is the situation we are now confronting, and it is a serious matter" (300a, 163f.).

10   Re: Rudolf Steiner's inner state in the last years of his work, cf. the many testimonies in my monographs, *Marie Steiner-von Sivers. Aufbau und Zukunft des Werkes von Rudolf Steiner.* Dornach 2006, pp.180ff and *Edith Maryon, Rudolf Steiner und die Dornacher Christus-Plastik*, pp. 117ff.

11   Cf. Gerhard Kienle: *Die ungeschriebene Philosophie Jesu.* In: Peter Selg, ed.: *Gerhard Kienle – Leben und Werk*, Vol. 2. Dornach 2003. Cf. also Rudolf Steiner's Michael address in Vienna in the autumn of 1923, where he says: "When we rise to a level where thoughts about spirit are as gripping as any physical thing in the world, we do so through the power of Michael. If we have the potential to receive thoughts of spirit, that power is what gives us confidence in such thoughts. We know that a particular impulse comes from spirit and that in devoting ourselves to it, we become the instrument of its implementation. If at first we do not succeed, it makes no difference. If we fail a second time, it makes no difference. Even if a hundred failures follow, they do not matter. No failure ever crucially impacts the truth of a spiritual impulse once we have seen and grasped its effect within. Having real confidence in a spiritual impulse that we have grasped at a particular point in time means recognizing that a hundred failures can prove only that the conditions for making the impulse a reality are not given to us in this incarnation. The character of the impulse itself, however, shows us that it is

correct. Even if the forces needed to implement a spiritual impulse grow strong enough only after a hundred incarnations, only the nature of the impulse itself can convince us that it will or will not ultimately prevail.

The human mind's greatest possible confidence in a spiritual impulse consists in holding fast to something we have recognized as spiritually victorious, holding fast and not letting go regardless of the outer world's condemnations. That is what the power and being of Michael wants from human beings. We may lay a spiritual impulse aside, even for an entire incarnation, but once we have grasped it, we can never waver in nourishing and cultivating it within ourselves. That is the only way to save it for later incarnations. That is how confidence in the spirit establishes a fundamental mood in our souls that enables us to recognize spirit as something as real as the ground beneath our feet—we know that if it were not there, we could not stand on it. When a spiritual impulse becomes this real for us, we sense what Michael actually wants of us.

No doubt you will admit that humanity has lost much of this active confidence in the spirit over the last few centuries or even the last millennium. Today, life does not encourage most people to develop such confidence, and that was something that had to happen" (223, 117ff.).

12   This lecture was first published in: *Beiträge zur Rudolf Steiner Gesamtausgabe*, Issue 88 (1985), pp 11-25 and was reprinted unchanged in: Rudolf Steiner: *Barometer des Fortschritts. Gesetze des sozialen Lebens.* Dornach 2006, pp. 95-124.

13   Re: Eisner's recommendation of Steiner, cf. Alwin Adolph Rudolph: "Erinnerungen an Rudolf Steiner und seine Wirksamkeit an der Arbeiter-Bildungsschule in Berlin" in: Johanna Mücke and Alwin Alfred Rudolph: *Erinnerungen an Rudolf Steiner und seine Wirksamkeit an der Arbeiterbildungsschule in Berlin 1899-1904.* Third edition, Basel 1989, p. 40; and Renate and Gerhard Schmolze: *Die Halbe Macht den Räten.* Cologne 1969, p. 7. Kurt Eisner (1867-1919), originally from Berlin, was a Social Democrat of Jewish descent who toppled the Bavarian king on November

7, 1918, and became prime minister of Bavaria, only to be murdered three months later, on February 21, 1919; cf. Bernhard Grau's biography of Eisner (Munich 2001). Rudolf Steiner had reviewed Eisner's essay "Psychopathia Spiritualis. Friedrich Nietzsche und die Apostel der Zukunft" in early 1893, immediately after its appearance. Through Emil Felber, his publisher in Weimar, Steiner sent Eisner his own *Philosophy of Spiritual Activity* in December 1893, asking that he discuss it "publicly" (39, 194f.). No documentation exists of Steiner's encounters with Eisner in Berlin at the end of the nineteenth century. Shortly before Eisner's death, however, their paths crossed again. At the end of the first week in February in 1919, Steiner talked with Eisner during the international Socialist conference in Bern. After Eisner was assassinated on February 21, 1919, Rudolf Steiner repeatedly mentioned Eisner's "Socialism and Youth," a lecture Eisner gave in the grand music hall in Basel on February 10, eleven days before he was shot and in "prescience of a tragic death" (193, 84). Steiner quotes him as saying, among other things, "Do I not hear or see clearly in the depths of our existence the life struggles of a longing that recognizes the life we must now live as quite simply and obviously the invention of some evil spirit? Imagine that a great thinker, living about two thousand years ago and knowing nothing of our times, had dreamed of how the world would look in two thousand years. Even with the most vivid imagination, he would not have thought of a world like the one in which we are condemned to live. In truth, what endures is the only utopia in the world; what we want, the longing that lives in our spirit, is the most profound and ultimate truth, and all else is dreadful. We are simply confusing dreaming with waking. Our task is to cast off the old dream that is society as it exists today. Consider the war: Can we conceive of any human rationality that could dream up anything like it? If this war was not what we call *real*, perhaps we have been dreaming and are now awakening" (193, 66).

14   Rudolph, op. cit., p. 32.

15 Cf. also the impressive description of circumstances in Berlin by Peter Weiss in: *Die Ästhetik des Widerstandes*. Frankfurt 1983, pp. 7ff.

16 Rudolph, op. cit., p. 42.

17 Johanna Mücke: "Erinnerungen an Rudolf Steiner aus den Jahren 1899-1904." In: Johanna Mücke and Alwin Alfred Rudolph: *Erinnerungen an Rudolf Steiner und seine Wirksamkeit an der Arbeiterbildungsschule in Berlin 1899-1904*, p. 20.

18 Rudolph, op. cit., p. 83f.

19 Mücke, op. cit., p. 18.

20 Rudolph, op. cit., p. 87.

21 For more on the bourgeoisie's failure, which began as early as the nineteenth century as a failure to take up idealistic liberalism and had exceptionally far-reaching consequences, cf. in particular Steiner's lecture of October 25, 1910 (185, 90ff.).

22 "This example is unique in the history of the human spirit: an unspoiled class of individuals, the modern proletariat, took up a scientific theory—Marxist teachings—with unspoiled and not yet decadent intellectuality, with full hearts and receptive souls, as if the forces at work in those teachings were their own life forces" (328, 50).

23 Cf. Rudolph, op. cit., pp. 70ff.

24 Mücke, op. cit., p. 87.

25 G. L. Dankmar: *Die kulturelle Lage Europas beim Wiedererwachen des modernen Okkultismus. Geistige, soziale und politsche Hauptströmungen*. Leipzig 1905.

26 Ibid., p. 23.

27 Ibid., p. 37.

28 Ibid., p. 34.

29 Ibid., p. 570.

30 Ibid., p. 574.

31 "A [state] church that acts as if the steel trust and the petroleum cartel are establishments ordained and personally instituted by the Lord God is digging its own grave. The official state church has always at least indirectly betrayed the downcast and the poor by preaching resignation to them,

while ultimately giving its blessing to every act of violence on the part of the mighty" (Ibid., p. 585).

32   Ibid., p. 579.

33   Ibid., p. 582.

34   Ibid., p. 588.

35   Ibid., pp. 594ff.

36   Ibid., p. 618f.

37   Similarly, Rudolf Steiner wrote in his essay "Theosophy and Socialism," published three years earlier: "First and foremost, those who want to intervene in a healing manner in social effects today need to learn something about the *causes* of those effects" (34, 435). And in an in-house lecture in the spring of 1905, he had said:

> Building a tunnel is an eminently practical matter. Suppose someone says that building a tunnel is easy: you simply have to start chiseling out a hole on one side of the mountain and continue until you get to the other side.
>
> Anyone can see the folly in this thinking, but in other aspects of life it is not so obvious. Of course if we intend to build a tunnel, we must first master the necessary higher mathematics and technology. Without the help of the practical science of engineering and knowledge of geometrically correct leveling, we would not be able to maintain the right direction when tunneling into the mountain. In addition, we must understand some basic principles of geology—rock layers, the direction of water flows, metal deposits in the mountain, and so on. It would be foolish to believe that someone with no knowledge of these things—an ordinary mason, for example—would be able to build an entire tunnel.
>
> It would be equally foolish to attempt to tackle the structure of human society from the standpoint of ordinary life, but many people—not to mention countless books—have committed that folly. Today everyone feels knowledgeable about and qualified to decide how best to reform the social order or the nation. People with almost no knowledge write detailed books about the best way

to configure society, and they also feel qualified to start reform movements. As a result, we have reform movements in all possible areas, but all of those efforts are like starting to build a tunnel with just a hammer and a chisel, because they are ignorant of the major laws that govern the world and originate in the life of spirit. The great misfortune of our time is due to ignorance that certain major laws apply to the structure of the human state and social body, just as there are laws that apply to tunnel-building. In order to perform even the most necessary daily functions in the social body, we must be aware of the relevant laws, just as we must be familiar with how all the relevant natural laws interact before we begin to build a tunnel. Before we even consider initiating social reforms, we must become familiar with the laws governing interactions in society. We must consider how souls influence other souls; that is, we must approach the spirit.

That is why theosophy must underlie all practical activity in life. Only those who take theosophical principles as their starting point for approaching life's practical aspects can feel qualified to be socially active. That is why theosophy should get involved in all branches of life. With no grounding in theosophical principles, politicians and social reformers, and the like, are nothing. That is why all of today's work on the structure of the social body is superficial piecework—complete chaos, to anyone with a real overview of the matter. To anyone who understands the situation, what today's social reformers are doing is like someone smoothing stones and piling them up in the hope that they will turn into a house all by themselves, when in fact the first thing we need when building a house is a plan, a blueprint. It is equally foolish, however, to expect aspects of society to take shape by themselves. We cannot reform society without knowing the laws of theosophy (93, n129ff.).

38   Cf. note 36.

39   Benediktus Hardorp: "Trennung von Arbeit und Ein-kommen?

Anthroposophische Perspectiven zu einer zentralen Gegenwartsfrage." In: *Arbeitslosigkeit. Ursachen und Auswege.* Stuttgart 1984, p. 87.

40   "The struggle for existence has become the slogan of [academic] research. [...] In the form of universal economic competition, this struggle has become an actual reality, right into the circumstances of individuals" (54, 41). On the situation of anthropologically and economically oriented social Darwinism in Steiner's time, cf. GA 54, 38ff and 179ff. "It is incumbent upon the future to reestablish brotherhoods— specifically, brotherhoods based on spirit, on the soul's highest ideals. [...] To work out of community is the secret of humanity's future progress" (54, 193).

41   As quoted in: *Beiträge zur Rudolf Steiner Gesamtausgabe,* Issue 88, 1985, p. 22.

42   Ibid., p. 23.

43   Hardorp, op. cit., p. 69.

44   As quoted in: *Beiträge zur Rudolf Steiner Gesamtausgabe,* Issue 88, 1985, p. 23.

45   Ibid., p. 22f.

46   Before World War I, examples of implementing the fundamental social law were attempted within the Theosophical Society: "Then the idea emerged to do something as a kind of sample or model" (337b, 151). For more information, cf. Alexander Lüscher's account (337b, 331f).

47   Christoph Lindenberg: *Rudolf Steiner. Eine Chronik. 1861-1925.* Stuttgart, 1988.

48   "Marx speaks of economic forces dominating even before the sixteenth century, but this is absurd, as I have demonstrated. Only in the sixteenth century did the economy moved into human affairs in the way Marxism conceives, and this trend then peaked in the nineteenth century. With regard to earlier historical times, ideal or spiritual impulses can be discussed very objectively, and it is possible to demonstrate how they have weakened in modern times in contrast to materialistic economic forces" (28, 377).

49   Diary of Count Otto Lerchenfeld, as quoted in Roman Boos,

ed.: *Rudolf Steiner während des Weltkrieges.* Dornach, undated, p. 58.

50 Cf. Albert Schmelzer: *Die Dreigliederungs-Bewegung 1919. Rudolf Steiners Einsatz für den Selbstverwaltungsimpuls.* Stuttgart 1991, pp. 59ff. Steiner emphatically described Wilson's "national self-determination" as problematic ("that unholy amalgamation of state, nation, and populace") and predicted its dramatic and tragic relevance for the history of Europe as a whole in the twentieth century ("nationalism is part of [an emerging] program that will be considered a blessing in the near future") (185a, 78). For more on this subject, see also Mark Mazower: *Der dunkle Kontinent. Europa im 20. Jahrhundert.* Berlin 2000, pp. 69ff.

51 Rudolf Steiner: *Geisteswissenschaftliche Erläuterungen zu Goethes "Faust."* GA 273.

52 For a Christological perspective on money's connection to the being, power, and activity of Ahriman, especially as illustrated in the third, "Ahrimanic" temptation of Christ, cf. Rudolf Steiner's lectures on the Fifth Gospel (GA 148) and my exploratory work, *Rudolf Steiner und das Fünfte Evangelium*, Dornach 2005, p. 88f. In 1964, Hans Erhard Lauers was the first to point out that Rudolf Steiner's formulation of the fundamental social law "signified nothing less than the response to that remnant of Christ's temptation by Ahriman that had gone unanswered at the time" (*Grundgeheimnisse des Christentums.* Dornach 1964, p. 64). Rudolf Steiner said, "And Christ Jesus knew that with regard to Ahriman, a remnant persisted that could not be overcome through any such inner, spiritual process *but only by other things that are still needed*" (148, 148; italics added). I emphatically concur with Lauer's view that the "remnant" of the third, Ahrimanic temptation that persisted at the beginning of the Christian era is intimately connected to developments foreseen and initiated by the fundamental social law (and the threefolding of the social body). Cf. also in this context a comment by Karl König: "Those who are forced sell their labor for money immediately and repeatedly become the successors of Judas." (*Über die Dreigliederung des sozialen*

Organismus. Föhrenbühl and Brachenreuthe 1964, p. 44).

53   Hans Georg Schweppenhäuser: *Das Soziale Rätsel XIII.* Freiburg 1979, p. 14.

54   In this context, cf. Steiner's functional definitions of "illness" and "healing" in my monograph *Krankheit, Heilung und Schicksal des Menschen. Über Rudolf Steiners geisteswissenschaftliches Pathologie- und Therapieverständnis.* Dornach 2004.

55   Rudolf Steiner: *Das Karma des Berufes des Menschen in Anknüpfung an Goethes Leben.* GA 172, lecture of November 12, 1916.

56   In Basel on April 9, 1919, Rudolf Steiner explained further: "In any social organism in which the division of labor prevails—that is, anywhere in the modern civilized world—egotistical work is an economic impossibility. We have no choice in the matter. Everything an individual does must accrue to the benefit of the totality, and everything individuals receive comes from social capital. After the introduction of money dissolved the natural economy and resulted in the further division of labor, this fundamental economic principle emerged: In a social organism in which the division of labor prevails, individuals cannot work for their own benefit but only for the benefit of others. In reality, working for our own benefit is as impossible as nourishing ourselves by consuming ourselves. You may say, "But what if someone is a tailor? If he makes a suit for himself, he is working for himself." In the context of a social organism characterized by the division of labor, however, that is not the case, because there the relationship between the tailor and the coat he makes for himself is completely different than it would be in a primitive economy. Today we have only enough time for brief explanations, not for fully valid proofs, so let me refer you to my book *Towards Social Renewal.* It is indeed possible to prove that if a tailor makes a coat for himself today, he does so in order to be able to work for other people. Today, that coat is produced not as an item for personal consumption but as a means of production. Its character has changed simply because the tailor is living in a social organism based on the division of labor. In everything

that happens in that society, economic altruism is at work. If we violate this principle—that is, if we attempt to encroach upon this legitimate social process by egotistically acquiring products that ought to flow into the community, we are actually giving birth to a lie, a real lie. The egotism of today's economic order is nothing more than a sum of lies or sins against what is actually going on beneath the service according to the law of social, economic altruism" (329, 170f.).

57 Rudolf Steiner's lecture in Stuttgart on February 2, 1921, provides his clearest description of the selfless perception and action that would be required by the "associations" he proposed. Among other things, he said: "Intelligent production depends entirely on knowing the needs that exist in a certain area. Goods produced in excess will inevitably sell for too little, and those produced in insufficient quantities will be too expensive. A commodity's price depends on how many people are involved in its production. The fundamental, vital issue for the economy is to start from meeting needs—in fact, meeting needs freely. This living process cannot be accomplished through statistics but only by an association of people from a particular area who know the needs of its population and are therefore in a position to negotiate—on a living, purely human basis—how many people need to be involved in the production of a particular item. The association must include people who cover a certain territory (with its boundaries determined on an economic basis) to inform themselves about existing needs and initiate negotiations about how many people must be involved in production in a particular branch of industry in order to meet those needs. It is important that the people assigned to this task allow needs to emerge freely, without in any way imposing their opinions as to whether some need is justified or not. They must limit themselves to objectively confirming needs as people perceive them. Combating pointless, luxurious, or harmful needs is not the responsibility of economic associative activity but is subject only to the influence of the cultural sphere. Pointless or damaging needs must be eliminated from the world through cultural instruction in refining

one's desires and sensations. An independent cultural life will certainly be able to do that. To give a crude example, education should discourage people from developing a taste for movies, but there should be no ban on movie theaters that is enforced by the police. That is the only healthy way to combat harmful influences in society. When either the government or the economy passes judgment on needs as such, we are dealing with a chaotic and confusing mix of cultural, economic, and other interests, not with the threefolding of the social body. Threefolding is a profoundly serious matter. Cultural affairs really must be allowed their independence. They are not free when any type of censoring agency can forbid anything that falls into the realm of human needs. If you are a fanatic, you can rail against movies as much as you like without impacting the independence of cultural affairs, but as soon as you call the police or insist that movies should be forbidden, you are impinging on that independence. We must keep this firmly in mind and not be intimidated by a certain degree of radicalism.

To begin with, therefore, the associations must include people who inform themselves about the needs existing in a certain area and then initiate negotiations (not make laws!) about what production is needed. Let's put it in more mundane terms for the sake of illustration: The associations will need objective agents who cannot be exclusively interested in selling the greatest possible quantities of the commodities they represent but must rather ask, what are the needs? These agents, who make up one element of the associations, must also be experts in determining how to organize production to meet these needs. The second element enlists transport providers who ship products and initiate negotiations to ensure those products get to where they are needed. The associations need consumption experts, distribution experts, and—as the third element—production experts. The production experts, however, come from the independent cultural realm, which includes everything that flows into the activity of production through human abilities. Expertise flows into production via instruction from the sphere of cultural affairs. So you see, associations in the economy will represent all three members of the social body. The associations themselves, however, will belong entirely to the economic sphere and deal only with economic affairs, i.e., with the consumption, circulation, and production of goods and with the related process of price-setting. That is why the threefold social body needs corporations with authority in only one of its members" (338, 167ff.).

58 Cf. Schmelzer, op. cit., pp. 113ff.

59 In the summer of 1919, in his essay "International Necessities of Life and Social Threefolding," Steiner wrote: "Historical circumstances resulted in national boundaries having little to do with the economic interests of the people who live within them. As a consequence, national governments establish international connections that would more naturally be established directly, by the people or groups of people involved in the economic activity. To acquire the raw material it needs from another country, an industry should not have to do anything more than negotiate with the administrative body responsible for that material, and all aspects of this negotiation should be confined to the economy itself. We can see that in recent times the economy has assumed forms that suggest such a self-contained status; national governmental interests are a disruptive element in this self-contained economic activity, which is gradually attempting to become a single global entity. What can the historical circumstances that gave England sovereignty over India possibly have to do with the economic circumstances of German manufacturers ordering goods from India? The catastrophe of the World War revealed that the life of modern humanity cannot tolerate disruption of the global economy, which strives for unity, by the interests of national territories (22, 22f.). Steiner tells us that "humanity's international activity" is striving for "complete separation in configuring cultural connections among peoples and economic connections among geographic areas" (24, 25). In Dornach, on March 22, he said, "The best way to forestall conflicts such as the one that broke out in 1914 is to administer international human connections in such a way so that one member must

engage in dialogue with the other. Just imagine how much more complicated it will become for two territories to go to war when a conflict between national governments requires the input of self-contained cultural and economic systems" (190, 44).

The year the war ended, Steiner was already describing with some urgency unavoidable future conflicts that would result if centralized nation-states survived. Speaking about economic developments in the Soviet Union, he said: "An economic territory attempting to develop in the governmental context of a collective society would be unable to maintain economically advantageous connections to foreign countries that still had capitalistic economies. Facilities that are administered like government agencies and subjected to a central economic administration deprive factory managers of opportunities to supply needed products to foreign countries. Even if these managers are left relatively free to accept orders, they are subject to the collective administrative authorities when it comes to procuring raw materials. In practice, they would find themselves caught between the needs of foreign customers and the internal administration's business policies, and the situation would eventually become impossible. Imports would experience the same difficulties as exports. To any unbiased view, this is sufficient proof that a geographic area attempting to run its economy according to abstract socialist principles cannot engage in fruitful commerce with capitalist foreign countries (GA 24, p. 26f.). Steiner clearly warned not only of the danger of communist "quasi-governmental organizational structures" but also of the equally dangerous tendency to form "super-states" and "super-parliaments," i.e., the de facto creation of one large economically and politically oriented state—a tendency that emerged suddenly after the end of World War II and is still shaping the fortunes of Europe (and the rest of the world) today.

60   In a lecture in Dornach on October 14, 1921, Rudolf Steiner pointed out that in spite of his agreement in principle to the distribution of an English translation of his book *Die*

Kernpunte der sozialen Fragen in den Lebensnotwendigkeiten der Gegenwart und Zukunft, this basic work would actually already need to be rewritten for English or American circumstances: "It is good that these ideas are being translated and disseminated, but as I said from the beginning, it would be most accurate and appropriate to rewrite this book very differently for America, and also for England. It would be very different from how it was written for Central Europe and Switzerland" (339, 65f.).

61 As early as 1917, Rudolf Steiner was concerned about the economic and materialistic power motives and intentions behind American propaganda about democracy saving the world. He wrote: "In its unmasked essence, the peace plan of Wilson and the Entente would read: 'We Anglo-Americans intend the world to be as *we* want it, and central Europe will have to acquiesce'" (24, 380).

62 In a previously cited essay from 1917 on the Chymical Wedding of Christian Rosenkreutz, Rudolf Steiner wrote: "Inasmuch as human beings regulate their *interactions in society* according to their ordinary consciousness, forces are allowed to intervene that do not favor humanity's healthy evolution. Confronting and counteracting these forces requires other forces that are derived from supersensible consciousness and incorporated into human interactions" (35, 349).

63 Cf. the summary of press reviews in *Beiträge zur Rudolf Steiner Gesamtausgabe*, Issue 88, 1985, pp. 7ff.

64 Cf. Schmelzer, op. cit., pp. 155ff.

65 Ibid, pp. 200ff.

66 Quotations taken from *Beiträge zur Rudolf Steiner Gesamtasugabe*, Issue 27/28, 1969, p. 27f.

67 Cf. Peter Selg: *Edith Maryon, Rudolf Steiner und die Dornacher Christus-Plastik*. Dornach 2006.

68 The "immaturity" argument was apparently quite common: "We encounter the strangest objections. One of the most frequent is: Well, threefolding would be very nice, but it would require different people" (331, 231). In a lecture in Stuttgart on July 2, 1919, Rudolf Steiner again emphasized that the

organizational forms he was proposing would literally foster maturity—i.e., that they had the potential to overcome egotism, as opposed to current structures that encouraged it. In that lecture, he said, "Anyone who makes such statements fails to grasp that much of what people express today is a consequence of our social circumstances and will change instantly as soon as those circumstances become healthy. [...] We must realize that improving social conditions would give people the opportunity to become better human beings. If we ask people to become better human beings *first*, however, there is no need to change those social conditions at all. If social conditions have not made people the way they are, then those conditions must be all right. Here you can see that the first, most basic need is to rethink and relearn certain things" (331, 231f.).

69   Italics added.

70   On related developments in the course of the twentieth century, cf. also Eric Hobsbawm's abysmal balance sheet: *Das Zeitalter der Extreme. Weltgeschichte im 20. Jahrhundert.* Munich and Vienna 1995.

71   Cf. also Rudolf Steiner's statement of February 11, 1906: "Hell is nothing other than complete ensnarement in personal concerns" (97, 33).

72   Cf. also Rudolf Steiner's early study on "Freedom and Society" (1898), which includes the following passage: "It is easy to demonstrate that when culture first developed, all social institutions sacrificed the interest of the individual to that of the totality. It is equally true, however, that in the further course of development individuals have attempted to assert their needs against those of the totality. On close inspection, a large part of history has consisted of individuals asserting themselves against communities that were necessary in the early stages of the development of civilization, communities based on undermining individuality. Healthy reflection will force us to acknowledge that social institutions were necessary and that they could come about only by emphasizing common interests. But the same healthy reflection also leads us to acknowledge that individuals must necessarily oppose the sacrifice of their

unique interests. As a result, over the course of time social institutions have assumed forms that increasingly make allowances for individual interests. In our own time, it seems safe to say that the most advanced individuals are striving for social forms of interaction that involve minimal constraints on the lives of individuals. Awareness of communities as ends in themselves is dwindling; instead, communities are meant to support individual development. The government, for example, is supposed to ensure that each individual personality has as much space as possible to develop freely. Arrangements for the common good are supposed to serve the individual, not the state as such. J. G. Fichte expressed this tendency in seemingly paradoxical but undoubtedly true words when he said that the purpose of government is to gradually render itself superfluous. An important truth underlies this statement. In the beginning, individuals needed community in which to develop their forces. Once these forces have developed, however, individuals no longer tolerate the community's paternalism. Each one thinks, I'll organize the community in the ways that best serve the development of my unique character. [...] In the early stages of culture, humanity sought to develop social alliances, and at first individual interests were sacrificed to the interest of these alliances. Further developments freed individuals from collective interests to develop their own needs and forces" (31, 253ff.).

73 Quotation from *Beiträge zur Rudolf Steiner Gesamtausgabe.* Issue 88, 1985, p. 20.

74 In a question-and-answer session in Zurich on October 28, 1919, Rudolf Steiner talked about the intrinsic connection between anthropologically based concepts of *work* and *will*. In particular—so Steiner tells us—these concepts must feature the perceptual quality of the processes of working and willing and the fact that both of these related activities are directed toward the individual's surroundings. "In the prevailing view of social economics, the most questionable concept is that of human work—a subject upon which I have already touched. I said that although the concept of labor plays a major role in Marxist theory, it is completely

misinterpreted there. As such, work or labor power has a social significance that is due to the product or the product's function in human interactions. A few days ago I said here that there is a big difference between physical activity for the sake of exercise and actual work—chopping wood, for example. When people chop wood, the significance of the activity lies in how their work flows into human community, not the expenditure of labor power as such. In the next few days we will see that we completely fail to do justice to work as a social function if we do not consider how it flows into the social body but view it simply as expenditure of energy. Now we may wonder, where do false concepts of work come from? If we view the so-called motor nerves correctly, we will also soon arrive at accurate concepts of how work functions in the social body. We must first realize that "motor" nerves are simply sensory nerves that exist to sense the nature of a limb to which the will conveys its energy. We will then discover how strongly any will impulse expresses itself in the outer world through work. An accurate concept of will and its relationship to the human body then serves as a foundation for seeing the relationship between will and work, and this idea then leads to accurate social concepts of work" (332a, 144f.). For more on the issue of "motor nerves" and human will, cf. also Wolfgang Schad (ed.): *Die menschliche Nervenorganisation und die soziale Frage*. 2 vols. Stuttgart 1992; and Peter Selg: *Vom Logos menschlicher Physis. Die Entfaltung einer anthroposophischen Humanphysiologie im Werk Rudolf Steiners*. 2 vols. Second edition, Dornach 2006. Vol. 1, pp. 174ff and pp. 334ff.; vol. 2, pp. 528ff. With regard to this concept of work in the context of the fundamental social law, it is important to note that according to Steiner, the process of human willing and moving extends beyond the human body into its surroundings: "Through willed activity, the soul extends beyond the domain of the body. In action, it participates in events in the outer world" (21, 158). Furthermore, the origins of human will impulses and movement are based on "the soul's direct association with the outer world" (192, 155)—in other words, on self-less initiative anchored in the world.

75 Cf. Hardorp, op. cit., p. 89: "From the perspective of rein-carnation, if encounters with other people are seen as steps on a shared path of development—perhaps even as steps and encounters *planned* before birth—payment for work acquires a different, rather negative meaning. For those involved, it arouses the possibly illusory impression that one person's output can be compensated by another person's money and that the two are "even" on the level of spirit and destiny once that work has been "paid for." From this perspective, the convention of payment for work may conceal essential aspects of our life and distract us from tasks we have set ourselves for this lifetime in connection with encounters with other people."

76 Cf. Selg: *Die Kultur der Selbstlosigkeit. Rudolf Steiner, das Fünfte Evangelium und das Zeitalter der Extreme.* Dornach 2006.

77 In Zurich on December 17, 1912, Rudolf Steiner com-mented indirectly on the connection between work "owed" to the community (see above) and the human capacity for love in performing work for others (see below). He said, "Ultimately, everything we do out of love is done to repay debts. From the occult perspective, anything done out of love does not bring payment but is itself compensation for something already consumed. The only actions that do not produce consequences for the future are the ones we perform out of real, true love" (143, 206).

78 Georg von Arnim, "Arbeit und Geld." In: Georg von Arnim: *Bewegung, Sprache, Denkkraft. Der geistige Impuls der Heilpädagogik.* Dornach 2000, p. 443.

79 In 1919, in an essay entitled "Die Zeitforderungen von heute und die Gedanken von gestern," Rudolf Steiner wrote: "In central Europe, the only thing that can lead to *healthy* progress is insight into the reconfiguration of all of orga-nized society." (Italics added.) In an essay on the Chymical Wedding of Christian Rosenkreutz, Rudolf Steiner formu-lated the inverse of this statement: "Inasmuch as human

beings regulate their interactions in society according to their ordinary consciousness, forces are allowed to intervene that do not favor humanity's healthy evolution" (355, 349).

80   "Antiquity anticipated future developments inasmuch as Mercury was already the god of commerce (the only independent aspect of economic life at that time), of physicians, and ... of thieves. (As Rudolf Steiner commented, 'The healer could also engender illness,' and so the mercurial element also encompassed the antisocial, thieving aspects of commerce.) The balancing element of healing will—not the will to equality—pours out into social life. Deeds of love pay off debts. Inasmuch as we are filled with responsibility for our fellow human beings, we become our brother's keeper." (Dieter Brüll: *Der anthroposophische Sozialimpuls. Ein Versuch seiner Erfassung*. Schaffhausen 1984, p. 195).

81   Cf. Selg: *Die Kultur der Selbstlosigkeit* and (as an example in the field of education) *Der therapeutische Blick. Rudolf Steiner sieht Kinder*. Dornach 2006.

82   As quoted in *Beiträge zur Rudolf Steiner Gesamtausgabe*, Issue 108, 1992, p. 46.

83   Cf. Selg, *Die Kultur der Selbstlosigkeit*, pp. 40ff.

84   Rudolf Steiner emphasized repeatedly that this "active living" in the "I" of the other is made possible by emotional participation in that person's life circumstances and destiny—or, in other words, "that compassion and love enable us to extricate ourselves from ourselves and actively live our way into the other being" (136, 69). Cf. also the corresponding information in Selg, *Die Kultur der Selbstlosigkeit*. Dornach 2006.

85   Ibid., pp. 31ff. Cf. also Rudolf Steiner's statement of December 19, 1910 in a lecture in Bern on the Matthew Gospel: "The community-building force through which human beings connect with other human beings is located in the ether body" (123, 254f.).

86   As cited in Selg, op. cit., p. 95f.

87   Willem Zeylmans van Emmichoven: *Der Grundstein*. Stuttgart, sixth edition, 1990, p. 78.

Literature Cited

Works by Rudolf Steiner referred to in the text and notes, listed in English when available.

All German titles are from the Rudolf Steiner Gesamtausgabe (GA), published by Rudolf Steiner Verlag, Dornach, Switzerland.

GA 10   *How To Know Higher Worlds.* Tr. Christopher Bamford. Hudson, NY: Anthroposophic Press 1994. *Wie erlangt man Erkenntnisse der höheren Welten?* (1904/05): 24th edition 1993.

GA 21   *Von Seelenrätseln* [The riddles of the soul] (1917): 5th edition 1983.

GA 23   *Towards Social Renewal.* Tr. Matthew Barton. Forest Row, Sussex, England: Rudolf Steiner Press 1999. *Die Kernpunkte der sozialen Frage in den Lebensnotwendigkeiten der Gegenwart und Zukunft* (1919): 6th edition 1976.

GA 24   *Aufsätze über die Dreigliederung des sozialen Organismus und zur Zeitlage* [Essays concerning the threefold division of the social organism and the period] (1915-1921): 2nd edition 1982.

GA 28   *Autobiography: Chapters in the Course of My Life.* Tr. Rita Stebbing, rev. Great Barrington, MA: SteinerBooks 2006. *Mein Lebensgang:* 8th edition 1982.

GA 31   *Gesammelte Aufsätze zur Kultur- und Zeitgeschichte* [Collected essays on culture and current events] (1887-1901): 3rd edition 1989.

GA 34   *Luzifer-Gnosis* [Lucifer-Gnosis: foundational essays on anthroposophy] (1903-08): 2nd edition 1987. The essay "The Education of the Child in the Light of Spiritual Science" is included in *The Education of the Child and Early Lectures on Education.* Tr. George and Mary

Adams Great Barrington, MA: Anthroposophic Press 1996.

GA 35   *Philosophie und Anthroposophie* [Philosophy and Anthroposophy] (1904-1923): 2nd edition 1984.

GA 36   *Der Goetheanumgedanke inmitten der Kulturkrisis der Gegenwart* [The Goetheanum-ideas in the middle of the cultural crisis of the present] (1921-1925): 1st edition 1961.

GA 39   *Briefe Band II* [Letters: volume II] (1891-1924): 2nd edition 1987.

GA 40   *Wahrspruchworte* [Truth-wrought words] (1886-1925): 8th edition 1998.

GA 53   *Ursprung und Ziel des Menschen* [The origin and goal of the human being] (1904/05): 2nd edition 1981.

GA 54   *Die Welträtsel und die Anthroposophie* [The riddles of the world and anthroposophy] (1905/06): 2nd edition 1983.

GA 55   *Supersensible Knowledge.* Tr. Rita Stebbing. Hudson, NY: Anthroposophic Press 1987. *Die Erkenntnis des Übersinnlichen in unserer Zeit* (1905/06): 2nd edition 1983.

GA 56   *Die Erkenntnis der Seele und des Geistes* [Knowledge of the soul and of the spirit] (1907/08): 2nd edition 1985.

GA 73   *Die Ergänzung heutiger Wissenschaften durch Anthroposophie* [The supplementing of the modern sciences through anthroposophy] (1917-18): 2nd edition 1987.

GA 83   *The Tension between East and West.* Tr. Dr. B.A. Rowley. Spring Valley, NY: Anthroposophic Press 1983. *Westliche und östliche Weltgegensätzlichkeit* (1922): 3rd edition 1981.

GA 93   *The Temple Legend.* Tr. John M. Wood. Forest Row, England: Rudolf Steiner Press 2002. *Die Tempellegende und die Goldene Legende* (1904-06): 2nd edition 1982.

GA 97   *The Christian Mystery.* Tr. James H. Hindes. Great Barrington, MA: Anthroposophic Press 1998. *Das christliche Mysterium* (1906/07): 3rd edition 1998.

GA 123   *According to Matthew.* Tr. Catherine E. Creeger. Great Barrington, MA: SteinerBooks 2003. *Das Matthäus-Evangelium* (1910): 7th edition 1988.

GA 135   *Reincarnation and Karma.* Tr. D. S. Osmond, C. Davy, S. and E. F. Derry. Hudson, NY: Anthroposophic Press 1992. *Wiederverkörperung und Karma* (1912): 4th edition 1989.

GA 136   *Spiritual Beings in the Heavenly Bodies and in the Kingdoms of Nature.* Original translation revised by Marsha Post. Great Barrington, MA: SteinerBooks 2011. *Die geistigen Wesenheiten in den Himmelskörpern und Naturreichen* (1912): 6th edition 1996.

GA 143   *Erfahrungen des Übersinnlichen* [Experiences of the suprasensory] (1912): 4th edition 1994.

GA 148   *The Fifth Gospel: From the Akashic Chronicle.* Tr. Anna Meuss. Forest Row, England: Rudolf Steiner Press 1998. *Aus der Akasha-Forschung. Das Fünfte Evangelium* (1913/14): 5th edition 1992.

GA 159   *Das Geheimnis des Todes* [The mystery of death] (1915): 2nd edition 1980.

GA 172   *Das Karma des Berufes des Menschen in Anknüpfung an Goethes Leben* [The karma of the vocation of the human being in connection with Goethe's life] (1916): 5th edition 1991.

GA 175   *Building Stones for an Understanding of the Mystery of Golgotha.* Tr. A. H. Parker. London: Rudolf Steiner Press 1985. *Bausteine zu einer Erkenntnis des Mysteriums von Golgatha* (1917): 2nd edition 1982.

GA 185   *From Symptom to Reality in Modern History.* London: Rudolf Steiner Press 1976. *Geschichtliche Symptomatologie* (1918): 3rd edition 1982.

GA 185a   *Entwicklungsgeschichtliche Unterlagen zur Bildung eines sozialen Urteils* [Evolutionary foundations for forming a social judgment] (1918): 3rd edition 2004.

GA 186   *The Challenge of the Times.* Tr. Olin D. Wannamaker. Spring Valley, NY: Anthroposophic Press 1980. *Die soziale Grundforderung unserer Zeit. In geänderter Zeitlage* (1918): 3rd edition 1990.

GA 187   *How Can Mankind Find the Christ Again?* Tr. Olin D.
Wannamaker, Frances Dawson, Gladys Hahn. Great
Barrington, MA: SteinerBooks 2009. *Wie kann die
Menschheit den Christus wiederfinden?* (1918/19): 3rd
edition 1982.

GA 188   *Der Goetheanismus, ein Umwandlungsimpuls und
Auferstehungsgedanke* [Goetheanism, a transformation-
impulse and resurrection-thought] (1919): 3rd edition
1982.

GA 189   *Die soziale Frage als Bewusstseinsfrage* [The social question as a question of consciousness] (1919): 3rd edition
1980.

GA 190   *Vergangenheits- und Zukunftsimpulse im sozialen Geschehen*
[Past and future impulses of social occurrences (1919): 3rd
edition 1980.

GA 191   *Soziales Verständnis aus geisteswissenschaftlicher Erkenntnis*
[Social understanding from spiritual-scientific cognition]
(1919): 3rd edition 1989.

GA 192   *Geisteswissenschaftliche Behandlung sozialer und
pädagogischer Fragen* [Spiritual-scientific treatment of
social and pedagogical questions] (1919): 2nd edition
1991.

GA 193   *The Esoteric Aspect of the Social Question.* Forest Row,
England: Rudolf Steiner Press 2001. *Der innere Aspekt
des sozialen Rätsels* (1919): 4th edition 1989.

GA 197   *Polarities in the Evolution of Mankind.* Tr. not known.
New York: Anthroposophic Press 1987. *Gegensätze
in der Menschheitsentwickelung* (1920): 3rd edition
1996.

GA 223   *The Cycle of the Year as a Breathing Process of the Earth.*
Tr. Barbara Betteridge and Frances Dawson. Hudson,
NY: Anthroposophic Press 1988. *Der Jahreskreislauf
als Atmungsvorgang der Erde und die vier großen
Festeszeiten* (1923): 6th edition 1985.

GA 260a   *Die Konstitution der Allgemeinen Anthroposophischen
Gesellschaft* (1924/25): 2nd edition 1987. See *The
Foundation Stone/The Life Nature and Cultivation of*

Anthroposophy. Forest Row, England: Rudolf Steiner Press 1996.

GA 262 *Correspondence and Documents. 1901-1925.* Tr. Christian and Ingrid von Arnim. Spring Valley, NY: Anthroposophic Press 1988. *Rudolf Steiner/Marie Steiner-von Sivers: Briefwechsel und Dokumente (1901-1925):* 2nd edition 2003.

GA 266/1 *Esoteric lessons (1904-1909) Volume I.* Tr. James H. Hindes. Great Barrington, MA: SteinerBooks 2007. *Aus den Inhalten der esoterischen Stunde.* Band I (1904-1909): 1st edition 1985.

GA 310 *Human Values in Education.* Great Barrington, MA: Anthroposophic Press 2005. *Der pädagogische Wert der Menschenerkenntnis und der Kulturwert der Pädagogik* (1924): 4th edition 1989.

GA 328 *Die soziale Frage* [The social question] (1919): 1st edition 1977.

GA 329 *Die Befreiung des Menschenwesens als Grundlage für eine soziale Neugestaltung* [Liberating the human being as the foundation for a new social form] (1919): 1st edition 1985.

GA 330 *Neugestaltung des sozialen Organismus* [The renewal of the social organism] (1919): 2nd edition 1983.

GA 331 *Betriebsräte und Sozialisierung* [Work councils and socialization] (1919): 1st edition 1989.

GA 332a *The Social Future.* Tr. not known. New York: Anthroposophic Press 1945. *Soziale Zukunft* [The social future] (1919): 2nd edition 1977.

GA 333 *Freedom of Thought and Societal Forces* Tr. Catherine Creeger. Great Barrington, MA: SteinerBooks 2008. *Gedankenfreiheit und soziale Kräfte* (1919): 2nd edition 1985.

GA 334 *Social Issues. Meditative Thinking & the Threefold Social Order.* Tr. Joe Reuter, rev. Sabine Seiler. Hudson, NY: Anthroposophic Press 1991. *Vom Einheitsstaat zum dreigliedrigen sozialen Organismus* (1920): 1st edition 1983.

GA 337b   *Soziale Ideen. Soziale Wirklichkeit. Soziale Praxis.*
[Social ideas, social reality, social practice] Vol. II (1920-1922): 1st edition 1999.

GA 338   *Wie wirkt man für den Impuls der Dreigliederung des sozialen Organismus?* [How does one work for the threefold social organism impulse?] (1921): 4th edition 1986.

GA 339   *Anthroposophie, soziale Dreigliederung und Redekunst* [Anthroposophy, the threefold social organism, and the art of public speaking] (1921): 3rd edition 1984.

GA 340   *Nationalökonomischer Kurs. Nationalökonomisches Seminar* [The National-economics course. Seminar] (1922): 5th edition 1996.

GA 343   *Vorträge und Kurse über christlich-religiöses Wirken II* [Lectures and courses on christian religious work, Vol. 2] (1921): 1st edition 1993.

b) Cited works by other authors.

Arnim, Georg von: "Arbeit und Geld." *Camphill Brief* 1969. Reprinted in: Georg von Arnim: *Bewegung, Sprache, Denkkraft*. Dornach 2000, pp. 435-444.
— "Das Soziale Hauptgesetz als sozialgestaltendes Prinzip." In: von Arnim, *Bewegung Sprache, Denkkraft*, pp 445-452.

Brüll, Dieter: *Der anthroposophische Sozialimpulse – ein Versuch seiner Erfassung*. Schaffhausen 1984.
— *Bausteine für einen sozialen Sakramentalismus*. Dornach 1995.

Götte, Fritz: "Das Soziale Hauptgesetz. Anlässlich seiner Formulierung durch Rudolf Steiner vor 50 Jahren." In: *Die Drei*, 6/1955, pp. 241-247.

Hardorp, Benediktus: "Trennung von Arbeit und Einkommen? Anthroposophische Perspektiven zu einer zentralen Gegenwartsfrage." In: *Arbeitslosigkeit. Ursachen und Auswege*. Stuttgart 1984, pp. 65-98.

König, Karl: *Über die Dreigliederung des sozialen Organismus*. 5 lectures, Föhrenbühl and Brachenreuthe, March 1964.
— *Die Mission des Gewissens*. Stuttgart 1992.

Kühn, Hans: *Dreigliederungs-Zeit. Rudolf Steiners Kampf für die Gesellschaftsordnung der Zukunft.* Dornach 1978.

Kugler, Walter: "Vor 66 Jahren: Driegliederungszeit." In: *Beiträge zur Rudolf Steiner Gesamtausgabe,* 88/1985, pp. 1-6.

Kugler, Walter and Rösch, Ulrich: "Die Gratwanderung zwischen Egoismus und Altruismus – 100 Jahre 'Soziales Hauptgesetz.'" In: *Rudolf Steiner: Barometer des Fortschritts. Gesetze des sozialen Lebens.* Dornach 2006, pp. 7-29.

Kannenberg-Rentschler, Manfred: *Die Dreigliederung des Geldes und das freie Geistesleben.* Dornach 1988.

Lindenau, Christof: "Eine Entdeckung Rudolf Steiners: Das soziale Hauptgesetz." In: Lindenau: *Soziale Dreigliederung. Der Weg zu einer lernenden Gesellschaft.* Stuttgart 1983, pp. 30-41.

Lindenberg, Christoph: "Der okkulte Aspekt der Arbeitslosigkeit." In: *Die Drei,* 4/1983, pp. 253-255.

Mücke, Johanna and Rudolph, Alwin Alfred: *Erinnerungen an Rudolf Steiner und seine Wirksamkeit an der Arbeiter-bildungsschule in Berlin* 1899-1904. Basel, 3rd edition 1989.

Müller-Wiedemann, Hans: "Zum Motto der Sozialethik." In: Steel, Richard and Rösch, Ulrich: "Das tun, was noch nicht da war." *Ein Lesebuch zu Rudolf Steiners Sozialem Hauptgesetz.* Dornach 2006, pp. 122-131.

Pietzner, Carlo: "Das Soziale Hauptgesetz in den Vereinigten Staaten." In: *Camphill Brief* 1969.

Schmelzer, Albert: *Die Dreigliederungs-Bewegung 1919. Rudolf Steiners Einsatz für den Selbstverwaltungsimpulse.* Stuttgart 1991.

Schweppenhäuser, Hans Georg: *Der soziale Auftrag der Anthroposophie und die soziale Verantwortung der Anthroposophen.* Freiburg 1972.

— *Das Soziale Rätsel XIII.* Freiburg 1979.

Steel, Richard: "The Fundamental Social Law – Background and Reality." In: Steel and Rösch, "Das tun, was noch nicht da war." *Ein Lesebuch zu Rudolf Steiners Sozialem Hauptgesetz,* pp. 110-121.

Tradowsky, Peter: *Frieden durch Krieg? Die Geisteswissenschaft als Friedensbewegung.* Dornach 2005.

Vobruba, Georg: *Entkoppelung von Arbeit und Einkommen. Das Grundeinkommen in der Arbeitsgesellschaft.* Wiesbaden 2006.

Werner, Götz: *Wirtschaft – das Füreinander-Leisten Karlesruhe 2004.*

— *Ein Grund für die Zukunft – das Grundeinkommen.* Stuttgart, 3rd edition 2006.

About the Cover Image

Freely you have received; freely give

The image on the front cover shows the third century itinerant healers, miracle workers, martyrs, and patron saints of physicians and pharmacists: Cosmas and Damian.

Cosmas and Damian were twin brothers, born in Egea, Cilicia, on what is today the coast of southern Turkey. Their mother was a pious Christian. From her, and through grace and their own labors, they acquired a deep faith in Christ. They were known as the Agioi Anagyroi or "Holy Unmercenaries" because they refused to accept payment for their works of healing: they strictly observed Jesus' words to the Apostles "Heal the sick, cleanse the lepers, cast out devils: freely you have received, freely give." (Mt. 10:8). Thus, too, they foreshadowed the first rule of the Rosicrucian Brotherhood: have no profession save to heal, and that gratis.

Cosmas and Damian practiced their work of healing first in the southern Turkish city of Adana, then in the Roman province of Syria, where they healed many and difficult cases. One of their most celebrated healings and a favorite subject for painters was what has been called "the first surgical transplant," in which they removed the diseased leg of an Italian man, and replaced it with the leg of a recently deceased Moor, "thus accomplishing, as well, the first interracial and cross-cultural healing..." (David Levi Strauss[1]).

During the persecutions by the Emperor Diocletian, Cosmas and Damian were arrested and ordered, under torture, to recant their faith. According to legend, their persecutors first tried to burn them, but the flames turned away and leapt onto their

---

1. David Levi Strauss, "In Case Something Different Happens: Joseph Beuys and 9/11," *Brooklyn Rail*, September 2011.

torturers. The same happened when they attempted to stone them: the stones turned back. Crucifying them and shooting them with arrows likewise failed. Finally, around the year 287, they were beheaded. They were buried in the Syrian City of Cyrrhus.

From the fourth century onward, word of their healings and martyrdom spread throughout Christendom. Their images appeared on countless healing icons, and many churches were named for them. In 527, Pope Felix (526-530) created the basilica of Santi Cosma e Damiani out of the Temple of Romulus in Rome by uniting it with the Forum of Vespasian, known as the "Forum of Peace," where the great Greek physician Galen was reputed to have lectured. Here the presence of Cosmas and Damian contrasted with and superseded Castor and Pollox, the remains of whose temple stood nearby.

Since then, at least up through the Renaissance, Cosmas and Damian, were a familiar part of Christian iconography and hagiography, representing the highest in human spiritual ethical practice. They were the patron saints of the Medici family and were depicted by, among others, Michelangelo, Donatello, Botticelli, Fra Lippo Lippi, Fra Angelico, Titian, and Rogier Van der Weyden.

Nor have they been forgotten today. In 1974, the German artist Joseph Beuys made his first visit to the United States. He was to give a series of lectures under the collective title "An Energy Plan for Western Man." Arriving in New York, he was fascinated by the recently completed Twin Towers of the World Trade Center. Presciently, he took a 3D postcard image of the towers, softened their angles and tinted them yellow, thus making them look, as David Levi Strauss notes in his description, like "two sticks of butter, a substance that responds to heat very differently than does crystal"; continuing: "The yellow also made the towers appear to be coated in sulphur, which in alchemy is the hot, dry, active seed of metals."[2]

Beuys then inscribed the two towers with the names Cosmas and Damian in blood red ink.

2. Ibid.

Ita Wegman Institute
for Basic Research into Anthroposophy
PFEFFINGER WEG 1 A CH-4144 ARLESHEIM, SWITZERLAND
www.wegmaninstitut.ch
e-mail: sekretariat@wegmaninstitut.ch

The Ita Wegman Institute for Basic Research into Anthroposophy is a non-profit research and teaching organization. It undertakes basic research into the lifework of Dr. Rudolf Steiner (1861–1925) and the application of Anthroposophy in specific areas of life, especially medicine, education, and curative education. Work carried out by the Institute is supported by a number of foundations and organizations and an international group of friends and supporters. The Director of the Institute is Prof. Dr. Peter Selg.